THEATRE IN FO[

CØØØ126633

VAUXHALL AND LONDON'S GARDEN THEATRES

by
John Dixon Hunt

Chadwyck-Healey
Cambridge and Alexandria VA

In association with
The Consortium for Drama and Media in Higher Education

First published 1985.

Chadwyck-Healey Ltd
20 Newmarket Road
Cambridge CB5 8DT
UK

ISBN 0 85964 161 9

Chadwyck-Healey Inc
1021 Prince Street
Alexandria, VA 22314
USA

CONTENTS

GENERAL INTRODUCTION

Theatre in Focus: A Pictorial History of World Theatre

Theatre in Focus is a new venture in publishing research in the field of theatre history. In 1974 the Consortium for Drama and Media in Higher Education introduced itself to the academic world by instituting a pilot project financed by the British Universities Film Council for two studies of Wilton's Music Hall and the Criterion, theatres whose buildings were at that date threatened with demolition. Each study took the original format of a set of slides illustrating the architecture of the theatre concerned and the styles of performance that went on there with an accompanying monograph which presented its research wholly in relation to the photographic evidence. The success of this venture encouraged the Consortium to develop the project into a substantial series.

The aim of the series is to cover three general areas of interest: notable theatres; particular actors, directors and companies; unusual theatrical *genres* and styles of performance. Special attention will be given to fields where audio-visual material is essential in teaching. Certain forms of theatre which are not rooted in a printable text pose considerable problems for the student and require an intense effort of the imagination if they are to be adequately visualised in terms of performance; and it is only in such terms that they can be properly appreciated. No volume in the series offers a detailed thesis on its subject, rather by ordering the material in relation to the illustrations each author seeks to enhance his reader's perception while leaving the reader free to shape the information that is offered to his own conclusions.

It is intended that, as the series develops, groups of sets should complement each other so permitting the composition of further monographs illustrating new themes, but using illustrations from existing sets. For example several commissioned sets devoted to aspects of popular theatre forms will make it possible to issue a monograph on Clowns and Styles of Clowning; while a further group of sets exploring the work of the theatre companies in Britain, America and the Continent in the Twenties and Thirties will provide material for a study of Expressionism. Monographs on theatrical design and styles of acting will also be included.

Each set comprises between thirty-five and fifty illustrations making accessible the best documentary evidence on the topic. The monographs include bibliographies of suggested further reading and frequently appendices giving secondary materials (architect's plans, important theatre-reviews, extensive descriptive accounts in novels or poems of particular buildings or performers) that are not readily available to the student of theatre.

Through the judicious and scholarly selection of the illustrations, through presenting his research entirely in terms of what those illustrations reveal, each author aims to bring the theatre of the past sharply into focus in his reader's imagination so that it becomes not simply historical fact but a living entity.

Richard Allen Cave *General Editor*

ACKNOWLEDGEMENTS

I am grateful to the staff of the various collections where research for this monograph has been carried out: the Harvard University Theater Collections, the Bodleian Library, the Museum of London and the Guildhall Library, London. I am also most grateful to Mr Brian Allen of the Paul Mellon Centre for Studies in British Art, London, for kindly reading and commenting upon a final draft and to Professor Kathleen Tillotson for helping me to a reference. Finally, I am most grateful to my student assistant, Anneke Tjan–Bakker, for her work on the final stages of this study.

LIST OF ILLUSTRATIONS

INTRODUCTION

Adieu to the pastoral Scene,
Where Harmony charm'd with her Call:
Where Pleasure presided as Queen;
In ye Echoing Shades of Vauxhall.

— Lockman

Hither Nymphs and Swains repair,
Quit the baleful scenes of strife,
Leave the rugged paths of care
And taste the joys that sweeten life.

from 'Invitation to Ranelagh', Arne

Many were the effusions in similar vein which celebrated the excitements of visiting one of the pleasure gardens of eighteenth-century London or which lamented leaving one after some particularly successful evening 'out'. When Jonathan Tyers opened Vauxhall Gardens on Wednesday 7 June 1732 with a *Ridotto al fresco*, he inaugurated the most famous and long-lasting of these open-air entertainments or garden-theatres. There were dozens of others (see slides 28–35), most of them springing up in imitation of Tyers's success, flourishing briefly as a novelty and then declining quickly; most, too, were of much more modest proportions and style than Vauxhall.[1] Its most interesting and renowned rival for many years was Ranelagh, which opened its Rotunda and Gardens on 5 April 1742. What distinguishes Vauxhall and (to a lesser extent) Ranelagh are their longevity – both continued into the next century, Ranelagh closing in 1803, Vauxhall as late as 1859 – and their ingenuity with establishing the gardens and related buildings as alternative *venues* to more conventional theatres.

Originally a plantation, prettily laid out with walks and arbours, Vauxhall always seems to have preserved its 'rural' appeal throughout the eighteenth century. From Jonathan Swift, who went to the New Spring Gardens (as Vauxhall was then usually called) in May 1711 to 'hear the nightingales',[2] to Horace Walpole who in 1769 thought that 'some thousand more lamps and a covered passage all round the garden . . . took off from the gardenhood',[3] its attraction was that it maintained an air of 'country'. This ambience was largely contrived by Walpole's time, sustained more by the pastoral songs and by the men hired by the management to lurk in the bushes and imitate the song of birds[4] than by any genuinely rural qualities. By the mid-eighteenth century the original glades had been criss-crossed by straight walks, diversified with sculptures and effects like the 'Cascade', which was activated each evening at nine o'clock after a bell had alerted clients to the event, with arcades and supper alcoves, a Rotunda, an orchestra and organ. The musical entertainments were augmented after 1745 with vocal contributions from some of the best musicians and singers of the day, from 1798 with firework displays and in the nineteenth century with an ever-increasing repertoire of circus and music-hall acts.

Ranelagh did not survive long enough for these more obviously theatrical elements to be added to its programmes. Its specially-built Rotunda and the walks and canals which had originally formed part of the gardens of the Earl of Ranelagh were the scene of concerts similar to Vauxhall's, promenades and – above all – masquerades. In the 1790s was added a representation of the eruption of Mount Ætna, with firework effects by the famous fireworker, Torré, and scenery by Marinari, 'painter to the Opera'.[5]

From such brief initial glimpses of the two great garden theatres of the eighteenth century, it will be immediately clear that this monograph offers a necessarily oblique view of theatre history. For it was only in the eighteenth century that Vauxhall became simply one stop on the London theatrical circuit for miscellaneous entertainers for whom stages and auditoriums were erected in the gardens.[6] Before the nineteenth century led Vauxhall into being, if a still rather eccentric, nonetheless a fairly straightforward alternative to the circus, concert or music-hall, its theatrical significance has to be registered in less conventional ways.

In the first place Vauxhall and the other garden-theatres of eighteenth-century London must be seen in the European tradition of both garden architecture and theatrical space (what Corneille called *le lieu théâtral*[7]). Gardens had been one of several locations for dramatic representations in the Renaissance before the permanent and indoor theatre as we now know it evolved. Those garden spectacles had almost always been courtly occasions, whether in Medici palaces, Versailles or English country houses on the route of a royal progress by Elizabeth I or James I. What Vauxhall, Ranelagh and other pleasure gardens provided for a much more mixed clientele was a popular and latterday version of those Renaissance traditions.

Moreover, garden architecture – partly as a result of the use of gardens for theatrical events – had developed various formal elements, such as *exedras*, alcoves, amphitheatres; these may have been used specifically as outdoor theatres, but many survived or were introduced into gardens without retaining that particular function. These 'fossils' of the garden's theatrical history were still invoked in the landscape gardens that were spreading through England during the heyday of places like Vauxhall. Their retention in Tyers's designs for his pleasure gardens, however, was another atavistic feature calculated to stimulate and enhance their theatrical atmosphere. All these traditions into which it is vital to put Vauxhall and Ranelagh are canvassed at more length below.

There is a further aspect of these garden-theatres which impinges upon social history and which connects the history of conventional theatres with larger aspects of English life. Together with the English landscape garden which was 'invented' and flourished in the eighteenth century[8] there was a similar and related vogue for 'conversation pictures'.[9] These paintings usually showed family groups in their gardens, which, as the century wore on, were frequently represented as landscaped in the newest fashion. Yet what these groups declare above all else is the presentation of themselves – family and property – as engaged in some social play or ritual. The landscape gardens in which they seem to take delight in performing their social roles are an apt (because modish) scenery for such display. So that even when the landscape movement seemed to make gardens more 'natural', they still retained a distinct theatricality – stages where aristocrats and (increasingly) a new middle class delighted to be seen. Vauxhall and Ranelagh partake clearly of this dominant theatrical strain of the age – a quality much commented upon by foreigners as well as by native writers, who often used Vauxhall or Ranelagh as settings which would underline what seemed to some of them an obsessive need to play-act in real life. Accordingly, no history of these London garden-theatres would be complete without some survey of their relationship, not only to theatrical history, but also to a social existence in which theatres extended their range from the conventional play-houses into other arenas. Vauxhall and Ranelagh certainly provided stages for professional entertainers; but they also offered 'scenes' – as the verses at the start of this introduction testify – for anyone who wished to act out in masquerade (or without costume) other roles than daily life habitually permitted. Hence the sequence of slides (14–17) which explore this social-psychological dimension of eighteenth-century theatricality.

Nevertheless, by the end of its life Vauxhall was making an important contribution to the fringe of London's legitimate theatre. No longer the fashionable resort of the past (compare Rowlandson with *Punch*, slides 23 and 48), it managed to retain popular audiences for its unique mixture of concerts, fireworks, ballets, balloon races, parachute descents (first by cats, later humans), marionettes, tight-rope displays, jugglers, recreations of the Battle of Waterloo and various cosmoramas and dioramic pictures. *Artistes* who performed at Vauxhall were also involved in regular theatre and music-hall events elsewhere, as were other theatrical personnel such as designers and entrepreneurs. Eventually Vauxhall succumbed to the competition from other *venues* which were better equipped to entertain a more and more demanding public. The English climate and Victorian morality also combined to drive Vauxhall out of business, for its largely out-of-door entertainments and rather seedy and disreputable audiences were respectively washed out by bad summers and sternly regimented by the local magistrates.

By July 1859, when what *The Times* called 'the old-fashioned gardens' finally expired and its tawdry and dilapidated paraphernalia realized £800 under the auctioneer's hammer, Vauxhall had established itself as a significant event in British theatrical history.[10] Together with other pleasure-gardens of London Vauxhall has been studied in the past rather more for its social and anecdotal interest and for the rich roster of personalities associated with it. As a consequence, other important aspects of its theatrical role, structure and tradition have been neglected.

COMMENTARY ON THE ILLUSTRATIONS

A   **VAUXHALL GARDENS: EARLY HISTORY AND MID-EIGHTEENTH CENTURY LAYOUT**

1   **A general prospect of Vaux Hall Gardens, shewing at one view the disposition of the whole Gardens**
(J. S. Muller, after Wale. Copper engraving from Stow's Survey of London, 1754. Robert Douwma (Prints and Maps) Ltd.)

A bird's-eye view of Vauxhall Gardens some twenty years after Jonathan Tyers inaugurated his management gives the layout of the gardens, seen from the south west, a layout which was basically never altered. It may be matched with a verbal account in *England's Gazetteer* of 1751:

> This [Fox-hall] is the place where are those called Spring Gardens, laid out in so grand a taste that they are frequented in the three summer months by most of the nobility and gentry then in and near London; and are often honoured with some of the royal family, who are here entertained, with the sweet song of numbers of nightingales, in concert with the best band of musick in England. Here are fine pavilions, shady groves, and most delightful walks, illuminated by above one thousand lamps, so disposed that they all take fire together, almost as quick as lightning, and dart such a sudden blaze as is perfectly surprising . . .[11]

In the foreground of Wale's view, taken in 1751, is the boundary wall nearest the river, with the manager's house, the former residence of Vauxhall House. Until about 1750 most visitors arrived by water, for boats waited at Westminster and Whitehall stairs to bring them up to Vauxhall –

> Lolling in state, with one on either side,
> And gently pulling with the wind and tide,
> Last night, the evening of a sultry day,
> We sail'd triumphant on the liquid way,
> To hear the fiddlers of Spring Gardens play,
> To see the walks, orchestra, colonnades,
> The lamps and trees in mingled lights and shades.[12]

After 1750 coaches could make the trip via the new Westminster Bridge; but the dangers from footpads and highwaymen, not to mention the confusion and traffic-jams on popular nights still made the land journey rather hazardous.

The most striking feature of the Gardens is the series of curving *exedras* divided into individual alcoves, some shown with supper tables laid. These colonnades are a crucial architectural component of Vauxhall's garden-theatre and will be considered in more detail later. Leading off the left-hand colonnade is the inside music room or Rotunda (with conical roof). In the central grove is the elaborate Orchestra, which inevitably reappears in other views, and behind it a similar structure. Of these two 'tents' a writer in the *Champion* who is possibly Henry Fielding, the playwright and novelist, wrote that they formed 'such a contrivance and form as a painter of genius and judgement would choose to adorn his landscape with'. While for its architecture and decoration he invoked Greece (it had Corinthian columns) and 'drapery far beyond the imaginations of the East' to capture the essence of this magical centre-piece.[13]

Three gravelled walks lead north east across the Gardens. The South Walk is decorated at intervals with triumphal arches and terminates in a grotto; at the near end, in the semicircle of supper boxes on the right is glimpsed the statue of Handel, which was erected in 1738.[14] About 125 feet to the left of the South Walk is the Grand Walk, leading from the entrance past the largest group of alcoves with the Temple of Comus at their centre. To the far right of the Gardens, narrower and more secluded, was the notorious Lovers' or Dark Walk. The main Cross Walk which traverses the Gardens immediately after the Orchestra grove and the first triumphal arch, led on the north (left) to a frame where transparent pictures were hung and illuminated. On the extreme left of the site is a fourth walk with wilderness on one side and on the other the 'Rural Downs', on which was placed a statue by Roubiliac of the poet Milton. This area and its special feature were described by a visitor in 1751: the 'Rural Downs' had

> little Eminences, after the Manner of a *Roman Camp*. In these *Downs* were three Openings, (last Season) covered with Shrubs, whence some styl'd them *the musical Bushes*, whilst others call'd the subterraneous Sounds heard there, the *Fairy Music*.
>
> These *Downs*, where Lambs are seen sporting, are cover'd with Turf; and pleasingly interspers'd with young Cypress, Fir, Yew, Cedar, and Tulip Trees. On one of the above Eminences in these *Downs*, is a Statue representing our great poet *Milton*, as drawn by himself in his *Il Penseroso*, seated on a rock; and in an Attitude listening to soft Music.[15]

It is a scenery that seems to owe as much to scene-painting in a contemporary theatre as to a taste for 'natural' landscape.

Somewhere along the walk beside these Downs was also placed a transparency of a Hermit seated outside his cave, presumably intended as an apt emblem for these more rural and private walks, but also doubtless related to Tyers's own garden at Denbies (see comment on slide 17) where he arranged his garden in a more sombre and moralistic mode than at Vauxhall where the public's pleasure was his principal concern.[16] Large paintings – resembling theatre backscenes, one of which was of a Chinese garden – terminated other cross walks. Immediately in the foreground of

Wale's view, with its white roof towards us and its (unseen) frontage towards the Orchestra, is the Prince's Pavilion, built expressly for Frederick, Prince of Wales.[17]

Before Tyers reopened and redeveloped the New Spring Gardens, as they were called for a while rather than Vauxhall (which was their location), the site had been less organized and less architectural. No views survive, unfortunately, of the Gardens prior to Tyers; but we know that the New Spring Gardens opened in 1661 – and were soon visited by John Evelyn, who thought it 'a pretty contriv'd *plantation*', and Samuel Pepys, who visited the 'ordinary house [i.e. refreshment room], and here we had cakes and powdered beef and ale, and so home again by water, with much pleasure'.[18] A Frenchman admired its regular, yet rural, aspect when he visited it in 1663:

> we crossed the Thames by boat to see two gardens, where everybody is able to stroll and to take refreshments in the taverns there or in the *cabinets* of the garden. They are called the *Springer* [sic] *Garden*, which means the Garden of Spring, of which that called the New is much more beautiful than the other. There I admired the grass walks and the smoothness of those which were gravelled. It is divided into a large number of squares, 20 or 30 paces across, enclosed by gooseberry bushes; and all these square plots are planted with raspberries, rose bushes, and other shrubs, as well as with grass, and with vegetables like peas, beans, asparagus, strawberries, etc. All the walks are bordered with jonquils, gilliflowers and lilies.[19]

Monconys was, however, probably misinformed about the name of the gardens. Their 'Spring' was not the season, but perhaps the *giocchi d'acqua* of water jokes which burst from concealed fountains either after a visitor stepped upon some trigger or as a result of being activated by a gardener hidden from view. John Aubrey reported that Sir Samuel Morland, famous for his hydro-mechanical skills, had constructed these fountains *al italiano* in the gardens of Vauxhall House;[20] but Morland's lease did not begin until after the gardens had opened. Since *giocchi d'acqua* were ubiquitous in Italian Renaissance gardens and much commented upon by foreign visitors,[21] it is conceivable that some existed before Morland's tenancy. But this original (if even supposed) connection with Italian garden art would be confirmed and augmented by later developments in the New Spring Gardens.

Other literary glimpses of the Gardens before Tyers's regime come mainly from Pepys, a great frequenter, from various Restoration plays and from Addison (see Appendix). The dramatists' allusions are especially interesting, since they suggest that at an early period Vauxhall became associated with intrigue, 'play' and experimenting with social roles.[22]

The title of *The Mulberry Garden* (1668) by Sedley invokes some rival gardens at Clerkenwell, but Vanbrugh's *The Provoked Wife* (1697) and Etherege's *She Would If She Could* (1668) both have scenes set at the New Spring Gardens. Lady Brute in the first thinks that they are an ideal location for her plot with Bellinda and she associated them with 'surprise . . . the most agreeable thing in the world'; the male libertines delight in the opportunities for intrigue which the gardens' walks and wildernesses allow, for as Ariana accuses them in Etherege's play – 'you seldom row out to Fox Hall without some such plot against the city'. The theatrical dimension of life in

Restoration comedies is thrown into especially high relief when the scenes are set in pleasure-gardens. At the end of *The Provoked Wife* IV iv Lady Fancyfull and her maid use an arbour in the New Spring Gardens from which to watch the others, who are themselves actors (Lady Brute and Bellinda) and audience (Constant and Heartfree), the deceiving and the duped; when that sequence is broken up by Sir John's drunken intrusion, Vanbrugh shows the roles subtly changing, as Bellinda and Heartfree go off to pry into the 'secrets of the Garden', as innocent spectators themselves now, while Lady Brute and Constant remain behind to rehearse another old social act.

Such theatrical presentations of these Gardens in contemporary drama must somewhat modify the lavish encomiums of Vauxhall's rural simplicities. Pepys, no mean adept at pursuing his amorous roles in New Spring Gardens – as witness his visit there on 23 April 1668 with the famous actress Mrs Knepp – was always charmed by its pastoral air: on 20 July he walked an hour alone, watching the 'citizens' eating cherries off the trees. Not the least, therefore, of the joys of New Spring Gardens was that, unlike the original Garden of Eden, fruit-picking was free and harmless.

This matrix of gardenist and theatrical motifs was maintained and augmented by Tyers after 1728, when he took the lease of the old House and Gardens at an annual rent of £250. He would later purchase the property in two lots (in 1752 and 1758). It remained in the Tyers family, managed after his death in 1767 by one of his sons, until 1821.

2   The Vauxhall Fan
(Both sides shown. Etching, printed in blue, 1736. H.R.H. The Prince of Wales, Duchy of Cornwall.)

This is the earliest reliable view of Vauxhall. It is taken from the Proprietor's House (in the foreground of the previous slide) and shows the simple, open supper boxes before their enclosure as alcoves; in the distance is the statue of Aurora. On the reverse side is represented the Prince of Wales's Pavilion. The lively encounters and characters of the Gardens are sharply depicted, especially on the side that shows the orchestra.

The fan was available from Pinchbeck's Fan Warehouse, and was one of the many souvenirs that Vauxhall promoted during its lifetime. There are various impressions and editions, some with different scenes: another impression of the scenes shown on this slide (in the British Museum) is lettered with the artist's name (M. Harris) and the date, '12 March 1736'.

For an almost contemporary literary account see *A Trip to Vauxhall* (1737) reprinted in the Appendix.

3   The Temple of Comus
(Engraving by Thomas Bowles after S. Wale, c.1751. The British Museum. Grace Collection, p.xxxv, sheet 45, 141.)

One of the several curved arcades in the gardens, this was terminated at each end with domed pavilions and in the centre by the so-called Temple of Comus. In effect, this rococo-Gothic-Chinese structure alludes only indirectly to Milton's masque, presumably its use for the reception of company being intended to recall Comus's celebration of 'Midnight shout, and revelry,/Tipsie dance, and Jollity'. It was newly completed in 1751 and had been decorated by the Flemish artist, Pieter Jan van Reysschoot, with the scene of *Vulcan catching Mars and Venus in a net.* Each of the supper alcoves to the side of The Temple of Comus, here seen laid for the meal or already receiving company, was also decorated with a painting as were most of the other alcoves later (see next two slides).

These curved lines of alcoves throughout the Gardens were a structure which both linked Vauxhall's design to earlier garden and theatre history and promoted the special brand of theatricality for which Tyers's establishment became famous. They were probably created in the late 1740s.

The apsidal shape of the pavilions echoed a standard form of Renaissance garden architecture, itself indebted to many readings and misreadings of classical ruins including theatres. John Evelyn, for example, remarked upon the 'theatre for pastimes' when he visited Carlo Fontana's strikingly scenographic climax to the gardens of the Villa Mondragone at Frascati.[23] Such apsidal structures were a basic device in Italian garden design from the earliest at the Vatican – Bramante's *exedra* in the Belvedere Courtyard, itself copied from the Temple of Fortuna Primigenia at Palestrina, which is itself now recognized as having been used for various ritual performances.[24] After the Belvedere, the shape of a concave wall, perhaps with niches, or even an alcove cut into the hillside, sometimes mounted by a series of steps, became a permanent feature of seventeenth- and eighteenth-century gardens in France and England; we shall encounter a famous English example, contemporary with Vauxhall, later (see slide 13). Vauxhall's curving pavilions, then, had many precedents in gardens and in the theatrical use or at least ambience of gardens. In practice, too, they created a semi-circular space which became the amphitheatre for society, a 'stage' to be viewed from the surrounding supper boxes. These niches were simply the adaptation to mass entertainment of garden alcoves and/or theatre boxes.

But there were other theatrical dimensions to this aspect of Vauxhall Gardens. The *exedra*, whether as intimate alcove or larger *frons scaenae* – Fontana's water theatre at Frascati has the air of such a classical 'proscenium' – had acquired an ambiguous status in garden design during the seventeenth century; this Vauxhall exploited with success. The scenographic garden which Evelyn enjoyed at Mondragone, for example, was both a stage – its statues and fountains viewed from the garden below – and *cavea* or auditorium from which the garden below could be viewed in turn. Visitors were therefore *both* spectators of a garden's dramas (statues, automata, waterworks, etc), often using theatrical language to convey their garden experience,[25] *and* actors in the dramas themselves, especially when they were trapped in the watery ambushes of *giocchi d'acqua.* Vauxhall's layout contrived a series of amphitheatres where its visitors were both watched from the boxes and themselves spectators of those within the supper booths. This theatricality is a dominant theme in all accounts of the Gardens and it will be discussed again in connection with other illustrations.

4   Engravings of four paintings in the Vauxhall supper boxes,
including 'Falstaff in the Basket'
(Guildhall Library.)

Of the fifty-odd supper boxes apparently forty-eight were decorated with a painting; these pictures, according to John Lockman in 1751/52, 'exhibit the most useful lessons of *Morality*, blended with the happiest strokes of Humour'.[26] They also contributed – which is more to our purposes – images of play and theatre.

Tradition gives to William Hogarth the suggestion that Tyers should open Vauxhall Gardens with a *ridotto al fresco*; Hogarth also contributed at least indirectly to the decoration of the gardens. His *Henry VIII and Anne Boleyn* (presumably a copy of the engraving) hung in the Prince's Pavilion and copies of his *Four Times of The Day* paintings were in another pavilion. Another painting, fragments of which survive, *The Fairies Dancing on the Green by Moonlight*, has also been attributed to Hogarth.[27] But the majority and possibly even *The Fairies* were the work of Francis Hayman, one of the group of artists who gathered at Slaughter's Coffee House and several of whom were connected with the Gardens (see variously below).

The paintings were scenes from plays and illustrations to romances; after 1740 incidents from novels and pictures of rural games and festivals were also featured. They represent a hugely important episode in British painting, which cannot be our concern here. But in their unaffected, lively mode they contributed a carefully contrived style and atmosphere to the Gardens; what Gowing has called their 'countrified' air is really an elaborately modified pastoralism – art artlessly imaging the country pursuits and pastimes which the citizens and visitors from the metropolis thought they were themselves enjoying when they made the trip to Vauxhall. Such, for example, are the subjects of *The Milkmaid's Garland* (now in the Victoria and Albert Museum), *Bird Nesting*, *Playing of Cricket* or *Bird Catching*.

A further series of pictures depicted various games: *Blind Man's Buff* or children on a see-saw or building a house of cards. From these it was a simple extension to depict adult games, both those like battledore and shuttlecock or quadrille and those social pastimes where 'play' of a less explicit kind is involved, as in scenes of *Fortune Telling with Coffee Grounds* or dancing round the maypole. When subjects from *Pamela* were added, the dramas of middle-class life as contemporary novelists like Richardson portrayed them took their place alongside scenes with theatrical figures like Falstaff (himself a compulsive role-player) or items of popular entertainment like Mademoiselle Catherina, a 'Puppet mov'd by Clock Work shown by the Savoyards for a Livelyhood'. They all contrived an ambience of make-believe and play, close to yet charmingly distanced from everyday life – which was the staple of Vauxhall's appeal. Hayman's experience as a scene painter for Fleetwood, the proprietor of Drury Lane Old Theatre, must have sustained this element of his work at Vauxhall. We know that visitors were attracted by the apparent realism of these large (8 × 5 feet) paintings, because the *Gentleman's Magazine* noted in 1755 that they had been touched up since the last season when they had been 'damaged . . . by the fingering of those curious connoisseurs, who could not be satisfied without *feeling* whether the figures were alive'. And this very role of intrigued spectator, viewing pastimes in which he would himself soon participate, was itself imaged in the first supper box, where 'Two Mahometans' were depicted 'gazing in wonder and astonishment at the many beauties of the place'; this picture was presumably meant to recall Addison's famous description of Sir Roger de Coverley's visit to the Gardens (see Appendix) which he thought a 'Mohometan Paradise'. The painting of the *Fairies Dancing*, as reconstructed by Lawrence Gowing, also has an awed rustic holding aloft his lantern to see the ring of dancers.

Paintings were installed also in the Rotunda Saloon, after it was enlarged in 1750–51 and decorated with 'four grand elegant Frames (with two smaller) made for *Pictures*', and in the Prince's Pavilion were various Shakespearean scenes. In all it must have been one of the most visited and admired public exhibitions of paintings ever seen in Britain. The subjects were first listed in a *Description*, published by Hooper in 1762, but various series of engravings had already given an even wider currency to the pictures than had the many visitors to Vauxhall. Examples of these popular reproductions are given here. As explained by Gowing, the engravings of Vauxhall paintings went through several phases, evidence of their popularity. Thomas Bowles published twelve in 1743 and two more in 1744, all of which bore titles and explanatory verses; the majority reversed the original subject. In 1743 Bowles put out a series of sea-pieces that had been painted for the Gardens by Peter Monamy. The original series was reissued, reduced in size and with four more subjects added. Some of Bowles's plates were reworked and published by Robert Sayer. In the *New Universal Magazine* between 1752 and 1754 small (6½ x 10½ inches) versions of Bowles's original issue were put out, and a collection of these devoted to the London pleasure-gardens was issued by Robert Sayer; being reversed again they present the images in the original sense. It is four of these, placed together upon one card in the Fillinham Collection at the Guildhall Library, that are shown here in order to present an adequate cross-section of Vauxhall subjects. As with the chequered career of the engravings, the original paintings did not always remain in the same place and were moved around the different locations. Gowing lists them in the order that both the *Description* (1762) and *The Ambulator* (1774) give.

5   **The Triumphal Arches down the South Walk at Vauxhall**
            (Muller, after S. Wale. Copper-engraving. 11¼ × 16 in. c.1760. Robert
            Douwma (Prints and Maps) Ltd.)

The Triumphal Arches, together with Roubiliac's famous statue of the composer Handel seen on the right, were further elements of the design of Vauxhall to give some theatrical scope to the Gardens. Triumphal arches, whether permanent and architecturally elaborate or temporary constructions, were a traditional element of courtly street theatre.[28] Vauxhall's arches, although themselves permanent, were nonetheless fabricated of wood and canvas on which columns were painted, like those which were erected to great princes upon their state entries into cities. Vauxhall's were, of course, far less elaborate in their decoration and doubtless more crudely rendered than those which had greeted, say, James I on his royal entry into London in 1604 or Charles II in 1661. But they seemed to have a similar effect: visitors reported on the 'peculiar air of grandeur' which they gave to the South Walk.[29]

The engraving communicates another striking effect, whereby the arches seem to invite visitors to explore the spaces that opened beyond them. Such spatial play had been a feature of Inigo Jones's masques and architectural designs in the early seventeenth century: scenes unfolded to disclose new vistas behind and beyond (even if illusionary), and archways were particularly effective in raising expectations of these further spaces. Jones's evident fondness for arches represents as much this wish to manipulate spectators as a predictable homage to Serlio's treatise on this kind of architecture.[30] We have other testimony on the effect of a series of doorways in drawing visitors into and through the excitements of a garden at Arundel House.[31] This tradition, then, of leading visitors on by means of arches and vistas was yet another revival and reaffirmation of old forms at Vauxhall.

Beyond the last arch could also be seen a distant ruin. In effect, this was a 'large and fine painting' set against the furthest edge of the Gardens, like some theatrical backdrop.[32] It represented the ruins of Palmyra, executed with sufficient realism to attract the visitor towards their sublime pile; the arches down the South Walk thus seemed 'like an entrance to a nearer view of those decayed structures of ancient grandeur'. In 1791 the ruins of Palmyra were replaced by a Gothic temple, which was illuminated on gala evenings and displayed an artificial fountain: 'The columns and chief part of the temple was a piece of curious machinery which kept in constant motion and formed a pleasing coup d'oeil'.[33] It seems in fact to have been simply a cheap and latterday version of those innumerable and ingenious mechanisms which so delighted English visitors in the grottoes of Italian Renaissance gardens (see slide 9). The effect of the arches and the distant prospect of the ruins or temple with the groves of the Gardens on either side recreated for popular tastes, then, a whole range of courtly spectacles; this particular vista may be compared, for instance, with the view of a theatrical performance in the grounds of Versailles, discussed later (slide 11).

In April 1738 Roubiliac's statue of Handel was installed in the Gardens and can be seen in this view on the right. Originally placed in a large niche on the southern side of the South Walk, its alcove was removed and the statue left as we see it here. Yet its first location and presentation were very deliberately theatrical: the 'proud alcove' had both an imitation curtain inside its 'proscenium' and a setting of real shrubs which formed (in the words of the *Gentleman's Magazine*) 'a Sort of woody theatre'.[34] It is a measure of the adjustments in Vauxhall's theatricality that this baroque manifestation at which a spectator simply gazed was replaced by a setting in which Handel was surrounded by the arena/auditorium of supper boxes, which has already been discussed. The statue was moved several times: in 1786 it was shifted to the back of the Orchestra, by 1793 it was inside the Supper Room, and in 1808 it was again out-of-doors in the grove behind the Orchestra. When one of Tyers's great-grandsons, George Rogers Barrett, inherited the gardens in 1809, the statue of Handel was removed to his house in Stockwell. It can now be seen in the Victoria and Albert Museum.

It is a striking piece, and not the least of its attractions today as in the eighteenth century is its informality. The composer is represented in loose disordered clothes and nightcap, with one stockinged foot rested on a discarded slipper; he is improvising on an Apollonian lyre, while a small boy transcribes the music; his left arm rests on various scores which are labelled ALEX FEAST, OPERAS, ORAS and LESSONS. Both the relaxed mood of the great composer and his association with theatrical ventures are surely emphases devised for Vauxhall. When Tyers announced the statue's installation in the newspapers he also told readers that he had subscribed generously to a recent Handel benefit night. The patronage of Roubiliac was another connection with the Slaughter's Coffee House group of artists, already involved in the decoration of the supper boxes.

6   **The Grand Walk at the entrance of the Gardens, and the orchestra with the musick playing**
(*J. Bowles. Copper-engraving. c.1760. Harvard Theater Collection.*)

7   **A view of the Centre Cross Walk**
(*E. Rooker (?) after Canaletto. 1760s. From grangerized* History of Vauxhall Gardens *(1890), I, 78, Harvard Theater Collection.*)

Two more views of famous vistas in Vauxhall Gardens. The Grand Walk, with the Orchestra to the right, would be the first prospect that a visitor had upon entering. Tyers inaugurated the 'grand Gothic orchestra' on 2 June 1735; though it underwent various refurbishments over the years – notably extra accommodation in 1745 for vocalists or 'an additional thousand lamps' – it apparently reached its final and much admired form by the end of the 1750s.[35] Its creator was a carpenter named Maidman, who decorated it with a concoction of his own devising like plaster of Paris and painted it gaily. It contained the organ and orchestra and – to judge from Rowlandson's watercolour view (slide 23) – was arranged at some date to accommodate supper boxes beneath. Details of its repertoire will be presented later.

The second view shows another of the Gardens' sumptuous and illusory backdrops, this time of the ruins of some Roman edifice; doubtless the engravings make it look even more realistic than it was. At night under illumination this vista must have had an impressive impact as visitors suddenly glimpsed it to their left moving up either the Grand or the South Walk. It nicely combines traditions from garden and theatre: for Batty Langley's *New Principles of Gardening* (1728) continued to advise garden owners to instal painted or real ruins as termination points to their walks, while London theatres apparently used imaginary or topographical items in their scenery.[36]

B   **THE HISTORICAL CONTEXT: THEATRES AND GARDENS**

8a   **Musicians performing for 'The Ballet of the Provinces of France' in the Gardens of the Tuileries, 1573**
(*Drawing by Antoine Caron, Fogg Art Museum, Harvard University.*)

b   **The amphitheatre of the Boboli Gardens, Florence, in 1637, during festivities to celebrate the marriage of Ferdinando II.**
(*Drawing by Stefano della Bella. Museo Topografico, Florence.*)

At this point it will be helpful to comment briefly upon some specific items from the early history of theatres, gardens and garden-theatres, which have been alluded to already.

They will show how fully Vauxhall Gardens exploited earlier traditions for a wholly different public.

Both these drawings show gardens being used by members of the Medici family for lavish entertainments. Long before the development of conventional theatres either within existing buildings like palaces (see slide 9) or as structures on their own, the Medici princes explored many other locations for their spectacular round of entries, festivities, marriage feasts and so on.[37] Among these, the courtyard and garden of their Pitti Palace were frequently exploited and, indeed, continued to be used for important public pageants right into the twentieth century. The amphitheatre was formed out of a natural declivity in the hillside to the south of the palace in imitation of the ancient Roman circuses; its architectural construction began in 1599. In the second image it is seen at a later date, with an elaborate and presumably temporary archway constructed at the ascent into the gardens behind; in the arena is a triumphal car and its attendants. The surrounding ranks of stone benches gave spectators who occupied them an excellent view of the performances, which included elaborately symbolic pageants, ballets and musical dramas, displays honouring the Medici or presenting neo-platonic visions, acted out by mythological characters. But anyone who explores the Boboli Gardens behind and to the right of this amphitheatre will quickly realize even today that the whole garden is some vast extension of those scenographic and metaphysical spectacles – in both its formal construction and its sculptural *dramatis personae* of classical figures.[38]

The dramatic entertainments of Italian Renaissance princes were copied through Europe – in England they increasingly determined the presentations before Elizabeth I and James I on their royal progresses, some of these held in gardens of castles and manor houses. And the masques which Inigo Jones and various collaborators devised for the early Stuart court, though invariably performed inside the Banqueting House or other buildings, testified with their frequent settings of gardens to their provenance in Italian and French out-of-door spectacles. The first image provides an example of the latter, showing the entertainment which Catherine de Medici staged in the gardens of the Tuileries palace in 1573 to honour the Polish ambassadors. The famous *ballet de cour* is shown at the point when ladies representing the sixteen provinces of France arrive at a specially constructed Mount Parnassus upon which Apollo and the Muses are seated playing their instruments.[39] As we shall see in the next slide such temporary erections for performances in gardens could also be realized as permanent features of princely gardens, complete with hydraulic shows.

One further idea connected with both Renaissance theatre and garden can best be explored here. When Evelyn exclaimed at the 'theatre for pastimes' on his visit to the theatre at the Villa Mondragone (see commentary on slide 3), somewhere in the background of his remark lurked a reference to the notion of *theatrum mundi*, the world itself as a theatre. Theatres like the Globe offered their audiences a microcosm of the world – indeed, the very fabric they watched with its painted heavens reminded them of this. Gardens, too, were expected to be a complete image of whatever world its local visitors would register – thus at the Medici villa of Castello north of Florence the gardens were designed to offer a complete image of the glory of the city and its rulers.[40] The words *garden* and *theatre* had come by the seventeenth century to mean complete collections or compendia. But if gardens and theatres were expected to register the world in its fullness, the world itself could be considered as a theatre, in which — depending upon the particular emphasis — human beings are the spectators of God's great drama or its actors.[41] The potential ambiguities of this view were exploited in both drama and gardens — visitors in the latter were certainly an audience but they could be involved and manipulated by a garden's spaces or dramas to such an extent that they also become its actors. We see something of this complex garden-theatre world in Caron's drawing of the Tuileries spectacle: members of the court are both actors and audience, the ballet itself represents not only the world of the French provinces but that rarer and more harmonious world of which Parnassus is the complete image. Such ambiguities of actor/audience we have already seen were endemic to Vauxhall Gardens, where the world came to perform and to see the world. Its rival, Ranelagh, was explicitly hailed as an epitome of 'the whole world in Miniature'.[42]

9a   **Mount Parnassus in the gardens of Pratolino with amphitheatre for viewing it**
           (Drawing by Gioanni Guerra. Late 16th century. Graphische Sammlung Albertina, Vienna.)
b   **View of the Villa Orselli at Marlia**
           (Engraving, c. 1755. Soprintendeza alle Galerie, Florence.)

Two examples of theatrical constructions in Italian gardens. Partly as a result of the use of gardens for dramatic performances (as in the previous slide), partly no doubt the more general effect of mannerist self-consciousness, Italian gardens came to be designed with elements clearly and closely related to theatrical usage. The Medici villa and gardens at Pratolino, north of Florence, were famous for the variety of grottoes and other ingenious contrivances which were activated for visitors by elaborate hydraulic machinery; the theatrical aspect of many of these was emphasized by their siting within some proscenium arch within which the scenes evolved.[43] One which did not have this format was the Parnassus Mount, on which Apollo and the Muses, presided over by the fabulous horse, Pegasus, played their instruments. This was drawn by the Modenese artist, Giovanni Guerra, who left a series of sketches of the gardens; in the first image here he shows the little semi-circle of seats for the audience of the Parnassus display, and he captions that portion of his sketch with 'Theatre to accommodate spectators for seeing and hearing'.

Further west, in the Duchy of Lucca, several villa gardens (as elsewhere in Italy) were furnished with outdoor theatres in the seventeenth and eighteenth centuries.[44] One constructed in 1652 out of green hedges can be seen on the extreme right of this site at Marlia (second image); it still exists. But it will also be noticed that the garden is elsewhere formed in quasi-theatrical shapes — immediately behind the villa itself are curving hedges backing a water theatre and another, more modest niche with temples or arches is located between the villa and the actual theatre itself. The formation of such gardens as these in shapes that immediately suggest theatres are part of the general and increasing theatricalization of art and life in the seventeenth and eighteenth centuries. Vauxhall is both heir to and adaptor and popularizer of these foreign and aristocratic examples, as much in its gardenesque and theatrical aspects as in its artistic and musical contributions.

10 Design for proscenium arch at the Teatro Barberini

(G. F. Grimaldi. Etching, 1658. Kungliga Biblioteket, Print Room, Stockholm.)

The development of indoor theatres (of the sort with which we are now familiar) necessarily involved the provision of scenery, and gardens came to feature prominently among the scenes provided. This was doubtless because many of the plays and operas had pastoral themes, for which garden landscapes seemed apt; but the contribution of gardens to *le lieu théâtral* before indoor theatres were fully established doubtless contributed to their popularity and frequency in settings.

Perhaps the best documented of European stage designers of this period is Giacomo Torelli (1608–1678). He was the first to create scenery for public performances of opera in Venice and in mid-career he went to France to provide settings for court operas and performances of such plays as Corneille's *Andromède* or Molière's *Les Fâcheux*, the latter presented in the gardens of Vaux-le-Vicomte in 1661 (see commentary on the next slide, 11). Torelli's designs confirm the incidence of garden scenes in seventeenth-century theatre: those he devised for *Bellerofonte* (1642) and *Venere gelosa* (1643) have elaborate arches set with statues, plants in pots and close-clipped hedges like walls; but for other works like *Deidamia* (1644) or *La Finta pazza* (1645) the designs suggest the invitations and excitements of garden spaces, illusionistically seen on painted drops.[45]

In the Torelli tradition is the design shown here. By Grimaldi for Marco Marazzoli's *La Vita Umana* (or *Trionfo della Pietà*), it shows the descent from a villa into its gardens painted on the curtain. However, the row of fountains across the front of the stage ran with *real* water rather than the usual cloth and tinsel imitation (still in use by Vauxhall's famous 'Cascade').[46] By using water piped from the gardens of the Palazzo Barberini to activate real jets in front of a *trompe l'oeil* garden scene the playful ambiguities of both theatre and garden are wittily maintained. *La Vita Umana* was presented as part of the Roman entertainments for Queen Christina of Sweden (whose arms can be seen on the proscenium). The theatre in the north west corner of the Palazzo Barberini had been erected in 1639 to designs by Pietro da Cortona; it seated 3,000.[47]

11   Grotto of Thetis, Versailles, during a performance of Molière's 'Le Malade Imaginaire' in 1674
(Etching and engraving by J. Le Pautre, from A. Felibien's Les Divertissements de Versailles . . . Paris, 1676. 311 B 14:2. Koninklijke Bibliotheek, Den Haag.)

The traditions and developments of Italian theatre and garden (intimately related, as we have seen) were translated northwards, partly as a result of designers like Torelli working beyond the Alps. The court of Louis XIV enjoyed spectacles and gardens of an unprecedented scale and grandeur, and it is one of many records of their conjunction that is shown here. The gardens designed by André le Nôtre at Vaux-le-Vicomte and then at Versailles often employed theatrical shapes and forms and these were used to stage plays and entertainments for the King; equally, the gardens as a whole could become the stage and setting for lavish *Fêtes*. In both respects Versailles was an aristocratic predecessor of Vauxhall, where the whole garden was a 'theatre' and also specific performances were presented at certain arranged locations within it.

It is one of these local stages at Versailles that is shown here. We have seen that at Pratolino the Medici grottoes had a distinct theatrical aspect, with hydraulic machinery producing 'events' from mythology to entertain visitors. At Versailles these traditions of theatrical grottoes were maintained, though on a much grander scale. Here the Grotto of Thetis has been transformed for a performance of Molière's *Le Malade Imaginaire* in 1674.[48] The Grotto itself was designed with clearly theatrical forms – the three niches with *tableaux* of Apollo and his horses can be glimpsed at the rear of the specially erected stage and their shapes and functions echoed in the sculptural decoration of the proscenium; equally, the triumphal arches which greeted the visitor on the outside of the Grotto are echoed in Apollo's niches and the proscenium opening – rightly, since all such performances were designed to enhance the *gloire* of Le Roi Soleil.

We must now follow these links between garden and theatre to England, but perhaps not without noticing how tenacious the relationship proved in Europe during the eighteenth century. In the 1740s the Margravine Wilhelmine created a fantastic garden, Sanspareil, west of Bayreuth: stories from Fénelon's *Adventures of Telemachus*, interwoven with stories from *The Odyssey*, are dramatized in various grottoes, one of which (dedicated to Calypso) was constructed as a ruined theatre with a perspectival series of decaying arches as the setting.[49]

12   Setting for first scene of Thomas Clayton's 'Arsinöe', 1705
(Sir James Thornhill. Victoria and Albert Museum.)

With some rare exceptions, set designs for English theatres in the period that concerns us here have not survived. What is available to us from verbal records (including stage directions in printed plays) makes it quite clear, however, that garden settings were a standard item in any theatre's repertoire.[50] They had been, of course, a feature of Inigo Jones's masque designs for the Jacobean and Caroline courts, a direct result of Jones's Italian experiences; and fortunately these do survive to show us his evident delight in gardens as territories for a masque's transformations.[51] But gardens also featured in the plays and operas of the Restoration, and (as I have discussed elsewhere[52]) garden settings seem to have brought with them into the theatre all the social and psychological opportunities which actual gardens of the seventeenth century provided.

Thornhill's designs for *Arsinöe* have attracted much attention from theatre historians, for their survival makes them something of a rarity. Attention has largely been focused upon the information they yield about stage conditions at the turn of the century.[53] What I would like to emphasize here is the role which such garden settings played in the opera's plot and themes (especially since one writer has claimed that the subject of the designs 'has little to do with this opera'[54]). The traditions of gardens are surely invoked by Clayton's opera – notably, their apt setting for heroic, ideal love and their potential for confusions. Thornhill's sketch for the first scene, shown here, is the setting for the Queen of Cyprus's slumbers and Ormondo's astonished discovery of her ('what heavenly Fair', he sings). His servant, stumbling around in the darkness, heralds the confusions that follow as Ormondo prevents the murder of Queen Arsinöe, pursues her attacker and leaves the Queen to flee in terror from the garden. Twice again gardens recur in the opera, reminders of an idyllic world of sleeping beauty and love at first sight. But the set of II.i is a 'Great Hall looking into a Garden' – affairs of state, resulting in Ormondo's fight with Feraspe, have pushed that world away into a distant prospect. II.viii brings the action outside once more ('Arsinöe alone. A Garden'); but it is her warring passions that she sings of and the garden's unstable paradise changes into despair and death as Ormondo is finally led off to prison.

The garden's associations with love (successful, frustrated or tragic), the uncertainties which its elaborate designs could playfully induce in visitors and its potential for dramatic event were exploited by comic dramatists. We have already seen how Restoration plays set in New Spring Gardens (the original Vauxhall) seemed to rely upon an audience's ready response to those aspects of garden life. Even if the settings were not as handsome as Thornhill's or the imaged garden quite so princely, British theatre-goers would have undoubtedly seen garden imagery and connected it with a theatricality of plot and stage behaviour as well as accepting garden settings as *de rigueur* in the contemporary repertoire. And as Sybil Rosenfeld has shown in her study of *Georgian Scene Painters and Scene Painting*, gardens continued to be a conspicuous element of theatrical productions. Aaron Hill's *Rinaldo* (1711) used real water for a cascade in the set for the enchanted garden; Handel's *Atalanta* had a specially designed garden set. Theatre managements also responded to the current *furor hortensis* by representing contemporary examples of the new English landscape garden in their scenery: Ranelagh appeared on stage, and *Oracle of Delphi*, a pantomime given at Sadler's Wells in 1799, had a Vauxhall set.[55]

13   **Claremont, Surrey**
(Unknown artist, after 1729. Oil on canvas. The National Trust. Photo: John Bethell.)

Just as theatrical sets for gardens by Inigo Jones or Thornhill derived their syntax and structure from continental models, so did gardens themselves. If English eighteenth-century gardens were not used as much as their Renaissance predecessors for theatrical entertainments, they did not lose all the forms and shapes originally connected with that function. The gardens designed by Charles Bridgeman at Claremont in Surrey contained a curious and striking 'theatre', seen on the right of this picture. It was a feature retained by William Kent when he redesigned the gardens in the late 1720s (the building on the island is by him).

Bridgeman's most recent commentator has nothing to say about either this theatre or the others of different shape that Bridgeman seems to have been fond of introducing into his designs.[56] Its exact purpose is unclear, except that it provided a platform from which to view the lower landscape (in this painting it is furnished with seats for the purpose). But what has never been noticed is that this typical Italianate structure (compare the platform at the Villa Mondragone, above, slide 3) actually uses a famous Italian design. Claremont's distinctive shape of a concave set of semi-circular steps giving place to a convex series which complete the descent was used by Bramante for the top of the Belvedere Courtyard in the Vatican and subsequently illustrated by Serlio in his architectural treatise; Bramante derived the form from the Temple of Fortune at Palestrina (the ancient Praeneste). Since we now know that this Roman temple was used for theatrical presentations, these curious steps have (probably coincidentally) a theatrical ancestry, which imparted a distinctive cast to the locations where they were used; doubtless as a result of Serlio's codification of the design, these double stairs were invoked frequently in European gardens. Their use at Claremont must be one of their last manifestations, an intriguing 'fossil' of earlier gardens' explicit theatrical functions.

| 14 | View of gardens at Hartwell House, Buckinghamshire |

14   **View of gardens at Hartwell House, Buckinghamshire**
(Bathasar Nebot, 1738. Oil on canvas. Buckingham County Museum, Aylesbury.)

15   **View of the parterre from the portico from 'Stowe Gardens in Buckinghamshire'**
(Jacques Rigaud, c.1734. Drawing. Metropolitan Museum of Art, Harris Brisbane Dick Fund 1942. 42.79[15].)

If the anonymous painter of Claremont did not show how its grass theatre was used by the inhabitants and their visitors – as an auditorium from which to watch the rest of the gardens, and perhaps as a stage on which they were watched by others below them – these two representations of Buckinghamshire gardens in the eighteenth century make such habits explicit.

Nebot's view of the bowling green and octagon pond at Hartwell House – one of a series of strikingly theatrical views of a very theatrically shaped garden[57] – suggests the different levels and the wings of tall clipped hedges which seem to make the people in it behave as if on stage. In this view five well-to-do persons perform their accustomed roles with self-confident gesture; they are watched by a couple to the right, while another scene is played by a further couple to an audience of one on the left. Since other parts of the garden were designed with extravagant wings and perspectival alleys (rural versions of the street scenes in Palladio's Teatro Olimpico in Vicenza), the behaviour of those we see in this scene seems entirely appropriate.

Rigaud shows a somewhat less stiff scene. Lord and Lady Cobham, the owners, are presumably the two seated figures, watching the activity on their parterre. I have often thought that the slightly hump-backed figure leaning on the chair may be intended as Alexander Pope, a frequent visitor who in his poems makes much of Stowe and other gardens as 'scenes' in which he and his friends play the rôles which his satires require of them. Here the Cobhams, whose famous and extensive gardens lay beyond the parterre, are the privileged spectators of an expansive scene; but they are themselves watched by their servants and guests who wander below them. The garden as a two-way theatre is clearly suggested by Rigaud's drawing even though his ostensible purpose is to record and glorify the gardens at Stowe and the idiom he adopts is close to the conversation picture.[58]

16   **Musical conversation piece with Frederick, Prince of Wales with his three eldest sisters**
(Philip Mercier, 1733, oil on canvas. National Portrait Gallery, London.)
17   **Jonathan Tyers with his daughter, Elizabeth and her husband, John Wood**
(Francis Hayman, oil on canvas, c.1750. Yale Center for British Art, New Haven, Connecticut.)

Whatever the actual dramatic purposes of those theatrical 'fossils' (as at Claremont) or theatrical shapes and structures (as at Stowe or Hartwell House), it is clear that gardens acquired the status of 'sets' or social stages in the conversation pictures which became such a favourite genre in the eighteenth century.[59] In these relaxed and often intimate scenes from daily life, however, we should not ignore the self-consciousness of both artist and sitters. The former is concerned to flatter both his patrons, their status and their public and private rôles (father, daughter, sister, etc). The sitters are usually seen in some room or garden belonging to them, so that pride of place and social status at once become part of the painting's subject matter. Their surroundings, seen in the most attactive light, are quite literally their stage, the theatre where they play their rôles, however those are conceived.

These two slides show different aspects of this mode. The Prince of Wales and his sisters, public figures, are here shown in a more private activity by the elegant and prolific conversation-picture artist, Mercier (there are three surviving versions of this scene alone).[60] We see them making music in the grounds of Kew with the Dutch House behind them (Frederick was leasing Kew House in 1733 and his sister Anne, usuaully taken to be the lady playing the harpsichord, was living in the Dutch House). We may gather something of the posed or theatrical gesture which Mercier aids his royal sitters in making if we note Frederick's garter insignia – an official, public item in this domestic scene. Furthermore, he and his sister Anne had reportedly been on such bad terms that they had not spoken to each other throughout 1733; yet the image of familial harmony, which their music making underlines, is a suitably public 'act' to perform for painter and public.

We may assume that Vauxhall's owner, Tyers, was not acting out a scene of domestic concord for Francis Hayman. Yet all three figures and their setting (almost certainly a *capriccio*) declare as much rôle-playing as did the royal group of sitters; Hayman's group is instinct with affection (the lap-dog, the symbolic amorino on the dolphin) and pride of family (the opulence of the landscape vista stretching behind and the richly wooded scene immediately around them). Nor can we really imagine that their poses are anything but contrived for this picture – a public performance by private persons just as the Prince of Wales and his sisters put on something of a private show.

Tyers might as well have been painted on his own country estate, Denbies, near Dorking in Surrey.[61] Here he created an elaborate moral landscape, employing the same artists – Hayman and Roubiliac – that were decorating the public pleasure gardens at Vauxhall. There was an eight-acre wood which Tyers called *Il Penseroso*; this was intersected by paths along which instructions and admonitions were designed to provoke suitably sombre thoughts. The most elaborate of these was the Temple of Death, filled with verses on the vanity, brevity and insufficiency of human pleasures. Beyond this Temple an iron gateway led to the Valley of the Shadow of Death, where further exemplary messages culminated in a large alcove 'forming an amphitheatre . . . entered through a portal made of grey Sussex marble'. Inside was a statue of Truth and two life-sized paintings by Hayman representing the *Death of a Christian* and the *Death of an Unbeliever*. It was to these pious scenes that Tyers went on Sundays from his residence at Vauxhall.

What we know of Denbies, which no longer survives, suggests that Tyers was fully aware of the rôle of setting in promoting behaviour; that the scenes of his country retreat and those which he arranged to entertain the public at Vauxhall presumably elicited very different behaviour simply points to the expectation that we adopt rôles according to the 'theatre' and 'play' in which we find ourselves or choose to act. But more importantly, as we end this survey of gardenist and theatrical contexts for the London garden theatres, it is useful to note that Tyers's 'amphitheatre' at Denbies, like the similar theatrical forms which evolved in the Vauxhall gardens, maintains the traditions of gardens as theatres; that the music making of Mercier's conversation picture and the social attitudes adopted in Hayman's are those pleasures which all sorts and conditions of men and women delighted to pursue at Vauxhall, Ranelagh and the other garden theatres of eighteenth-century London. To these we can now return, to trace the explicit theatrical history of Vauxhall especially. But the entertainments which Vauxhall provided – music, masquerades, fireworks, acrobats and so on – cannot ever be divorced from its larger theatrical aspects which this excursus has outlined.

C   VAUXHALL'S EIGHTEENTH CENTURY ENTERTAINMENTS

18   Vauxhall tickets
(Engraved from the original medallions by James Stow. Published 1825. The Museum of London.)

Admission to the *Ridotto al Fresco*, with which Tyers opened the Gardens in June 1732, was by ticket, priced at one guinea. In the *Daily Journal* and the *Daily Courant* of 31 May where Tyers made a preliminary announcement it was stated that 'no persons whatever to be admitted with swords, or without a printed ticket'. Evidently Tyers expected the worst, for he posted a detachment of one hundred Foot Guards around the Gardens. In the event everything went off quietly. Printed tickets continued to be used for admission, the usual price of which was one shilling; the price was only raised, to two shillings, in 1792, and then in 1809 to three shillings and sixpence, in 1821 to four shillings, after which prices were reduced. There were special admission charges for gala nights. After some abuse of the printed ticket system, entrance in 1736 was obtained simply by paying at the entrance.

Season tickets were available and for some years took the form of silver tokens struck from designs by William Hogarth; these were eventually replaced by printed cards. Hogarth himself was rewarded for his advice and assistance in decorating the Gardens with a golden ticket which allowed him and his friends perpetual admission ('In perpetuam Benefici memoriam' was inscribed upon one side). This token, together with other season tickets to the Gardens, is seen here in a nineteenth-century engraving.

19   'The Adieu to the Spring Gardens'
(Bickham after Gravelot. Copper engraving, 1737. Guildhall Library.)
20   'Rural Beauty, or Vauxhall Garden'
(Bickham after Gravelot. Copper engraving, c.1737. Robert Douwma (Prints and Maps) Ltd.)

Orchestral and then vocal music was the staple entertainment at the Gardens during the eighteenth century. Many famous lyric writers, composers and singers worked expressly for Tyers and subsequent managements. Frank Kidson rightly called the eighteenth-century London pleasure gardens 'the nurseries of English Song',[62] for they maintained the traditions of native song in the face of the modish inroads of Italianate opera and developed the literary and dramatic aspects of English song in directions that would lead eventually to the music-hall.

The songs, especially in the early days, were 'puffs' for the Gardens and their attractions. They would allude, as does *The Adieu to the Spring Gardens* of slide 19, to its various 'Splendours'; or they would rehearse the happy idea of setting out for a visit there, as did the anonymous verses which were published in folio the same year as Lockman and Boyce's song:

> Last Night, the Evening of a sulky Day,
> I sail'd, triumphant, on the liquid Way,
> To hear the Fiddlers of *Spring-Gardens* play;

To see the Walks, Orchestra, Colonnades;
The Lamps and Trees in mingled Lights and Shades.
The Scene so new, with Pleasure and Surprise,
Feasted awhile our ravished Ears and Eyes.[63]

But every good thing has its ending, and the song illustrated in slide 19 laments the necessity of departing from the Gardens or abandoning them entirely as a place of resort at the end of the summer season. The partnership of Lockman and Boyce makes this lament into a light, mythical confection, which the engraving by another member of the Slaughter's Coffee House group, Gravelot, makes somewhat more substantial with its images of a typical Vauxhall company; yet these doubtless flatter Vauxhall's clients too, with an elegance and decorum which were not always conspicuous. It must be the earliest picture of Vauxhall.

Another song of the same period, also with words by Lockman and music by Boyce, is *Rural Beauty*. Its verses refer to various attractions of the Gardens, another elegant image of which crowns the printed song-sheet. The first stanza (printed within the music lines) alludes both to Vauxhall's pastoral ambience by invoking Flora, the goddess of flowers, and to its fashionable appeal by calling to 'Belles and Beaux'; the second stanza gestures toward the supper alcoves, the third to the orchestra, the fourth to the famous illuminations, and the fifth summarizes the glamorous pastoral invitation by mentioning the classical imagery of mirth and celebration. The rococo decoration around the image and lyric aptly catches the light and frothy tone of Lockman's song, a typical and fine example of the musical fare which Tyers offered his patrons.

The principal soprano at Vauxhall in the late 1730s was Miss Stevenson, who performed many of Lockman's other songs, including that set to music by Gladwin and entitled *The Invitation to Mira, requesting her company to Vaux Hall Garden*. Among her successors was the tenor, Lowe, who made famous the song, *Jenny of the Green*, with which the new season of 1752 opened. Its printed sheet was headed with an image of a young man declaring his passion for a lady on the terrace of some elegant mansion, complete with urns and a fountain – precisely the blend between a stage scene and a conversation picture which has been discussed (see commentary on slides 10 and 14–17).[64] Other famous singers who appeared at Vauxhall, each making some new ditty the hit of the moment, were the coloratura soprano Miss Wright, the handsome Ann Catley, who made her debut at Vauxhall in 1762 before being engaged to sing both at Covent Garden and also at the rival Marylebone Gardens (see slide 31), Mrs Cecilia Arne, Mrs Wrighten, Miss Wewitzer, Arrowsmith who was the butler to the Lord Mayor's sword-bearer who provided funds for Arrowsmith's musical tuition, and Joseph Vernon. (For some comments on later artistes see slide 27.)

21   **The inside of the elegant music room in Vauxhall Gardens**
        (H. Roberts after S. Wale. Copper engraving, c.1760. Robert Douwma
        (Prints and Maps) Ltd.)

Partly to offset the disadvantages and unreliability of the English climate, partly to embellish the site and so keep up with the rival attractions of Ranelagh (see slide 29),

Tyers constructed the Rotunda on the north side of the Grove during his major refurbishments of 1749–50. Situated behind the row of supper boxes that the visitor saw upon his entrance to the Gardens, the Rotunda was given a Gothic main portal which faced the Great Walk. It was first known as the New Music Room or Great Room. J. Lockman's *A Sketch of Spring Gardens, Vaux-Hall, in a letter to a Noble Lord* [i.e. the sixth Lord Baltimore], published probably in 1752, describes it at length. He says the Rotunda was

> 70 Feet in Diameter; an Edifice fram'd in the highest Delicacy and Taste. The Roof or Ceiling is adorned with grand painted Festoons of Flowers, terminating in a Point; and looks like the Dome, if I may so speak, of a most august, royal tent . . .[65]

The walls were designed to imitate mosaic by an artist called Moser and can be seen in this engraving after a drawing by Wale. Lockman went on to describe

> 16 Sash *Windows*, the Frames whereof, (design'd by a very able Artist, to whom the *Rotunda* owes many Embellishments,) are in an elegant Style of Carving, (each *Window* being crown'd with a Plume of Feathers, the Crest of His Royal Highness the PRINCE OF WALES;) as were likewise the Frames of 16 oval *Looking-Glasses*, with two arm'd sconces.

Lockman makes a special point of noting how visitors could see themselves reflected sixteen times in these mirrors, to their 'pleasing wonder', and thereby participate in the illusion that they too had joined the ranks of 'eminent Personages, antient and modern' who were represented in '16 fine white *Busts*, standing on carv'd Brackets' beneath the windows. What is not represented in this image is the 'grand Chandelier', perhaps because it would have obscured the view of the passage-way to the annex; this held seventy-two candles, was eleven feet in diameter and at some later stage was decorated with a plaster of Paris representation of Jupiter's rape of Semele.[66]

So popular was the Rotunda that it was extended eastwards in 1751. This necessitated some reorganization of the Rotunda itself, and the orchestra, which originally occupied the east side where Wale shows a screen of columns, was moved to the opposite side (in other words to the point from which Wale drew the scene). This new orchestra was lavishly decorated, as again we learn from Lockman: it was

> inclos'd with a Balustrade, between a Screen of splendid *Columns* . . . On the Ceiling of this *Orchestra*, *Venus*, and the little Loves are painted; as are, on the Sides, Corinthian Columns, between which four Deities in Niches are represented. At the Extremity of the *Orchestra* is an *Organ*; before which stand the Desks [of the musicians].

But this new orchestra was itself moved, since by 1762 it was replaced by a plaster statue of Apollo on a plinth of wood.[67] The Rotunda seems to have been extensively redecorated for important occasions or to stimulate popular interest in the gardens: in 1785, for instance, it was 'rendered superb' by a transparent picture by Hamilton which showed the Prince of Wales in the armour of St George, surrounded by four female figures.[68]

The annex to the Rotunda, usually known as the Saloon, was similarly decorated and subject to *ad hoc* refurbishments. Lockman again provides an extensive description for Lord Baltimore. It was about seventy feet long and thirty-four feet wide and was approached from the Rotunda via

> a Screen of Columns, in a very grand style of Architecture. These columns are embellish'd with Foliage, from the Base a considerable way upwards; and the remaining Part of the Shaft, to the Capital (of the *Composite* Order) is finely wreath'd with Gothic Balustrade, where Boys are represented ascending it. Within this added *Room*, are ten three-quarter *Columns* . . . The Architrave consists of a Balustrade; the Freeze [sic] is enrich'd with sportive Boys; and the Cornice supported by Women, in the Form of *Terms* . . . In the eliptical [sic] arch'd Roof . . . are two little Cupolas in a peculiar Taste. The Summit of each is a Sky-Light, divided into ten Compartments, glaz'd; and the Frames are in a pleasing Gothic Style . . .

From the centre of each cupola hung 'a noble *Chandelier*, in the Form of a Basket of Flowers'.

This annex or Saloon was, like the supper boxes outside, used for the display of paintings. Between the ten columns, five on each side of the room, were frames 'made for *Pictures*' (according to Lockman), while the two cupolas were embellished with representations of Apollo, the Muses with Pan in one, and Neptune, with sea-nymphs in the other. In the early 1760s the four large frames between the columns were filled with canvases by Hayman depicting scenes from the Seven Years War. The first showed the surrender of Montreal to General Amherst; the second, Britannia, with a medal of George III, on the right-hand of Neptune; the third, Lord Clive receiving the homage of the Nabob of Bengal; and the fourth showed Britannia again, this time distributing laurels to the leading officers of the war (these included the Earl of Albemarle and the Marquis of Granby). There were mixed opinions of the pictures' success: some thought Britannia in the fourth picture looked drunk and the conduct of the allegory shoddy; Carl Philip Moritz, however, found the expression of the passions in the protagonists so moving that 'it affects you so much that you even shed tears'.[69] (For the stage and circus arena in the Rotunda, see slide 39.)

22   Spring Gardens, Vauxhall
(Etching and engraving by M. Romano, published by G. Bickham, 1741. Guildhall Library.)

Published as a frontispiece by Bickham (who used Romano as a pseudonym), this print is similar to Gravelot's (slides 19 and 20). It satirizes various activities and frequenters of the Gardens. Tyers himself is there (second from left), Lockman and Sir Robert Walpole, the fattish figure at left centre who points to the supper party around the table.[70] The verses underneath the image claim that visually it says all that needs to be said:

> Here you see Gallante Shewee;
> Picture plainer Speak then Prosee,
> of Vaux-Hall Gardens tout nouveauee.

Nevertheless, it is worth commenting further upon two items of the scene: the lamps, which it shows prominently over the supper boxes to the left and arched over the receding walk; and the supper itself.

Refreshments were always available at Vauxhall. The figure standing fourth from the left holds a knife and fork and is identified in the verses as a chaplain: whether part of the satire requires a clerical gentleman is not clear; but it is extremely apt that a parson who would hope to augment his living with free meals from his patrons is grasping eating tools, for Vauxhall meals were notoriously mean and costs not particularly low. In 1782 Moritz, previously quoted in connection with the Saloon paintings, found Vauxhall much more expensive than Ranelagh. A list for 1762, twenty years before his visit, gave the following prices:

Burgundy, a bottle	6 s.	
Champagne	8	
Frontiniac	6	
Claret	5	
Old hock, with or without sugar	5	
Two pounds ice		6 d.
Rhenish and sugar	2	6
Mountain	2	6
Red port	2	
Sherry	2	
Cider	1	
Table beer (quart mug)		4
A chicken	2	6
A dish of ham	1	
A dish of beef	1	
Salad		6
Cruet of oil		4
Orange or lemon		3
Sugar for bottle		6
Ditto for one pint		3
Slice of bread		1
" " butter		2
" " cheese		2
Tart	1	
Custard		4
A cheese cake		4
A heart cake		2
A Shrewsbury cake		2
A quart of arrack	8	

The *Literary Gazette* of 1817 was still remarking upon the stiff prices and gave the following instances:

	s.	d.
A quart of arrack	7 s.	
Two small chickens and a small quantity of ham	11	
A lettuce 'under the denomination of a salad'	1	6 d.
Six or eight cheese-cakes and biscuits	4	6
Wax lights	2	
Bread and beer for a party of four or five	4	

The thinness of the ham and other carved meats was proverbial; slices were as thin as muslin (it was given out that one of the carvers was so efficient that he could cover the entire surface of the Gardens from one single ham) and the chickens minute ('A chicken at best, is not a big bird – Id est – if it's bought at Vauxhall'). The punch, however, was exceptionally strong, and maybe as a consequence its cost did not rise as sharply as those for the food. To give some idea of the quantities consumed at one of Vauxhall's special masquerades, Southworth cites the supply by a Mr Ward of New Bond Street of the following items on 20 July 1812:[71]

> 150 dozen fowls
> 150 dishes of lamb
> 200 tongues and hams, ornamented
> 300 lobsters
> 100 raised pies
> 100 Savoy cakes
> 250 dishes of pastry
> 300 jellies
> 400 quarts of ice cream
> 500 pottles of strawberries
> 300 cwt. of cherries, besides a vast variety of other fruits which formed the
> dessert.

Perhaps in deliberate contrast to the thin ham, the lamps were hung in profusion. George Cruikshank made special mention of them in 1835:

> And remember the lamps, – how they're clustered
> By thousands and thousands of dozens;
> And then the dark walks – how I'm fluster'd,
> To think of your dearest cousins.[72]

Alas for the romance and intrigues of those unlighted walks, the magistrates ordered their illumination in 1825. Some years later oil was replaced by gas, which gave off too dazzling a light to be conducive to Vauxhall's long-established atmosphere of romance and which therefore may have contributed to the final demise of the Gardens. Nevertheless, successive managements tried hard to maintain this part of the Vauxhall tradition: in 1841 there were supposed to be 30,000 lamps, of which 4,000 alone were in the orchestra.

23 'Vauxhall Gardens'
(Thomas Rowlandson. Watercolour, 1785. Victoria and Albert Museum.)

Found in a junk shop in 1945, this marvellous evocation of Vauxhall Gardens is by one of the shrewdest commentators on the late eighteenth-century social and aesthetic scene. It was aquatinted by Jukes and etched by Pollard in the years immediately following its painting and the image enjoyed a widespread audience.[73] What is most striking, as David Coke has recently explained,[74] is Rowlandson's implied contrast between the natural and artificial: 'between the coarseness of humanity and the elegance of the architecture, between the dark of the night and the light of the lamps, between the various classes and types of people, and even the implied contrast between the human orchestra and the music supplied by the 'Feathered Minstrels' [i.e. birds] that were such a feature of the place'.

Rowlandson also catches precisely that degree of social play-acting for which Vauxhall provided the perfect stage, and he does so without recourse to the grotesque visual satire that sometimes accompanied images of masquerade costumes (see slides 25 and 26). The persons he represents, as we shall see in a moment, were famous and known in 'every-day life'; yet here they can be seen allowing themselves both that extra little dimension of licence because they are being watched by the *hoi poloi* and that modicum of role-playing which their finding themselves in the Gardens always authorized.

The singer in the box is Mrs Weischell, famous for the song 'Pitty-Patty'; beside her, the leader of the orchestra, F. H. Barthelemon, and peering out from between them, its conductor and organist, James Hook, remembered best as the composer of 'The Lass of Richmond Hill'. But the company seem far more intent upon their own performances than upon the music. In the box at the left is a distinguished group of literary folk: James Boswell, an unidentified man, then Samuel Johnson – a great friend of Tom Tyers, son of the original proprietor and immortalized as Tom Restless in the pages of *The Idler*, then Mrs Thrale, and finally Oliver Goldsmith (although in 1785 he was already dead). Goldsmith's account of the Gardens is reprinted in the Appendix. But it is perhaps Boswell's testimony that Vauxhall was 'peculiarly adapted to the taste of the English national' by being a mixture of 'curious show', 'gay exhibition', 'music . . . not too refined for the general ear', and 'good eating and drinking' that serves best as a motto for Rowlandson's view.[75]

Below the orchestra, hand on hip, is Edward Topham, journalist and fashionable spark; he gazes across at Mary Robinson, the lady being ogled by the Prince of Wales (wearing the Garter Star) in the centre of the right-hand group. She was a noted actress, having been spotted by David Garrick who organized her appearance as Juliet at Drury Lane, a role which was followed by other Shakespearean ones; that of Perdita in *A Winter's Tale* became her nickname. She was taken up by the Prince in 1778. At the extreme right, seated with two clients, is Mrs Barry, 'the Old Bawd of Sutton Street'.

Of the other company the most interesting is Georgiana, Duchess of Devonshire, one of the leading members of society. To her right (our left) is the elderly Admiral Paisley with a wooden leg; to her left, Lady Duncannon. From behind the tree against which Lady Duncannon is leaning peers the Rev. Sir Henry Bate Dudley, an aggressive journalist and since 1772 editor of *The Morning Post*; his articles provoked many opponents into challenging him to duels, hence his nickname of the 'fighting parson'.[76] Bate Dudley was involved in at least one fracas at Vauxhall itself, giving ample proof (if any were needed) that the disreputable and even dangerous side of the Gardens was not necessarily confined to the lower class riff-raff who had the wherewithal to gain admission. A set of verses from 1773 doubtless exaggerated the extent of the hooliganism:

> For certain every knave's that's willing,
> May get admittance for a shilling;
> And since Dan Tyers doth none prohibit,
> But rather seems to strip each gibbet,
> There is no wonder that the thief,
> Comes here to steal a handkerchief.
> For had you, Tyers, each jail ransacked,
> Or issued an insolvent act,
> INVITING debtors, lords, and thieves,
> To sup beneath your smoke-dried leaves . . .'

Bate Dudley was a friend of Garrick, and with his tartan-clad neighbour, James Perry, beside him adds a theatrical dimension to the scene. The radical journalist Perry had once been a provincial actor, till his strong Scots accent grew too much for the audiences. But these figures, with their theatrical connections, and 'Perdita' Robinson with hers only serve to underline the wholly theatrical atmosphere and series of social performances which Rowlandson both celebrates and – by slight caricature and sly sexual jokes – satirizes.

24 The inside of the lady's garden at Vauxhall

(Etching, hand-coloured, published by S. W. Fores, May 1788. Print Collection, Lewis Walpole Library, Yale University.)

This lively scene has been attributed to Kingsbury.[78] With slightly more distortion than Rowlandson employed, the artist has captured the affectations and preenings of female visitors. The elaborate hats, especially that of the second lady from the right, suggest the sartorial efforts which an appearance at the Garden elicited; they are at least half-way towards the masquerade concoctions discussed in slides 25 and 26. The lady who prepares her face for the amorous encounters outside this enclosure regards herself in a mirror, a preparatory moment of self-regard which will be repeated endlessly during the evening in either the mirrors of the Rotunda or the admiring glances of other visitors. That there was a lady's garden at Vauxhall is not surprising: it was the equivalent of the more recent Powder Room; but it was also a necessary retreat where the metamorphoses of the female visitors, as valued a part of the entertainment as the endless transformations of the Rotunda or 'scenes' around the Gardens, could be undertaken. By the 1770s certain leading costumiers who hired out masquerade costumes maintained changing rooms at Vauxhall and Ranelagh 'to prevent the inconvenience attending ladies and gentlemen getting in and out . . . with their Dresses on'.[79] Maybe this drawing depicts part of such a dressing room.

The dropped glove, fan and papers (whether programme or admirers' *billets-doux* is not clear) suggest a disorder which is rectified before leaving this female sanctum. One of the papers seems to say 'O'LEEKE VENEREAL', which would imply perhaps a patent cure for a disease which certain clients of the Garden caught or passed on; perhaps, therefore, these are whores, preparing themselves for the evening's work.

25   A masquerade at Vauxhall
('After a drawing by Lady Diana Beauclerk'. Watercolour, 1782. Guildhall Library.)

Apart from the musical entertainments, Vauxhall was popular above all for its masquerades. This long-established European habit of disguising one's everyday self in some specially chosen disguise at carnival time was adopted with particular success by London society during the eighteenth century. The Swiss count, Heidegger, introduced masquerades or masked balls at the Opera House in the Haymarket after his arrival in England in 1708. He was later created Master of the Revels by George II, a role he played with distinct success despite the satires directed at him by such as Henry Fielding:

> So for his ugliness more fell
> Was H–d–g–r toss'd out of hell.
> And in return by Satan made
> First Minister of Masquerade.[80]

The evils of the masquerades soon led to them being proscribed, though they continued to prosper under different names, like 'convocations' or 'ridotto'. *Ridotto* was an Italian word signifying haunt, retreat, foyer or green-room; its use maintained the theatrical characters of these assemblies. Tyers opened Vauxhall in 1732 with a *Ridotto al fresco*, at which many people wore dominoes – loose cloaks with masks covering the upper part of the face; these were also much worn in 1786 when the Gardens chose to celebrate their Jubilee.

Masks were not always allowed in the early years, though they were permitted on special occasions. This drawing suggests something of the contrived exoticism whenever masks were permitted. In a shady arbour are three masked figures, with others behind who thus throw into relief the fashion in which the foreground figures have withdrawn into a brief privacy. It is a charming and naive image of events which were celebrated more proficiently in publicly sold engravings (see next slide). Above all, it underlines what a commentator of 1774 called the 'odd, antic and whimsical dresses' which the 'people of fashion' adopted on these occasions.[81] But even when masquerades *per se* were not being worn some exoticism of dress – as the previous slide made clear – was still the order of the evening.

26a   Miss ———— in the actual dress as she appeared in the character of
Iphigenia at the jubilee ball or masquerade at Ranelagh
(Engraving, 1749. Bromhead Collection, London University.)

b   Rural masquerade dedicated to the 'Regatta'ites
(Engraving, 1776. Bromhead Collection, London University.)

Both Vauxhall and Ranelagh were popular for masquerades, but the latter seems to have, in its shorter existence, attracted more publicity, even notoriety. The first image shows Miss Elizabeth Chudleigh, maid of honour to the Princess of Wales; she shocked the town by appearing at Ranelagh in 1749 as Iphigenia. The costume was so scanty that the witty Mrs Montagu remarked that her 'dress, or rather undress, was remarkable; she was Iphigenia for the sacrifice, but so naked, the high priest might easily inspect the entrails of the victim'.[82] In the 1770s, when the craze for masquerades reached a new height, a Captain Watson appeared in the 'figure of Adam' with an 'unavoidable indelicacy of the dress' that was 'the contempt of the whole company'.[83]

The graphical idiom of the engraving, drawing upon representations of the *commedia dell'arte*, together with the caption of 'as she appeared in the character of', suggests the strong theatrical tone of these masquerades. Miss Chudleigh even appears upon what looks like a stage with trees as wings. As early as 1728 Henry Fielding satirized the dizzy range of characters who might be represented at a masquerade:

> . . . here, in one confusion hurl'd,
> Seem all the nations of the world.
> Cardinals, quakers, judges dance;
> Grim Turks are coy, and nuns advance.[84]

The long-established idea of *theatrum mundi*, already touched upon in the commentary upon slide 8, acquired a new and potent life in these masquerades: men and women from the whole of society acted out the parts of all nations and conditions. These were occasions, too, for inventive dialogue, for as Boswell noted they required 'a great flow of Spirits and a Readiness at Repartee'. And on some occasions, in order to stimulate the repartee, actors from the theatres were employed.[85] Fielding's last line, quoted above, hints at the incongruities which arose when a masquerader's 'lines' and behaviour clashed with his or her chosen *persona*.

The fashion for masquerades, as Aileen Ribeiro has noted, brought into being both masquerade warehouses and a whole social journalism. In the 1770s newspapers and magazines published long accounts of masquerades and costumes that were worn at them. Especially in the area around Covent Garden it was possible to buy or hire fancy dress: a notable store was Paulin's in Tavistock Street.[86] But patterns for such costumes were also available in books such as Thomas Jefferys's *A Collection of the Dresses of Different Nations* (1757).

Masquerades were often the occasion for dresses with overtones of political or social satire. The second image displays one of the absurdly constructed pieces of head-gear dedicated to the river races which were a feature of Ranelagh. There were Regatta Balls, with special Regatta songs[87], and when these ceased after 1775 there were rowing and sailing competitions held on the Thames. The lady's headdress shows both the races and the spectators who could use the gardens as a viewing stand. In 1775 a special temple of Neptune was constructed in the grounds.

The sartorial repercussions of such Ranelagh events are both demonstrated and satirized by this engraving. One such towering creation reportedly contained a ladder by which a frizzeur could ascend to maintain his handiwork, while Samuel Rogers recalled in his *Table Talk* going to the Ranelagh Gardens in a coach with a lady who wore such an enormous height of headdress that she was forced to sit on a low stool.[88] Tradesmen advertised their silver Ranelagh silks and Ranelagh waistcoats in gold, silver and colours. Indeed, the Macaronis, men with high toupet, nosegay and quizzing glass – for the ostentation and inventiveness of costume was (as with today's punk rockers) not confined to the ladies – suggest that the impulse to dress up for masquerades invaded the larger social life of the metropolis.

27   A collection of songs
(Engraved titlepage, 1796. Guildhall Library.)

The song industry connected with Vauxhall and other London garden-theatres was enormous. The popularity of some items meant (as we saw in slides 19 and 20) that they were issued as single sheets. Others, as here, were collected, their sale guaranteed both by their composer, Hook, and the famous singers who made them popular in the first place. And, as happens with items in the hit parade today, one success required another to displace it and to keep a clientele enthralled with old favourites as well as with the likelihood of new winners.

The music for these London gardens is a subject for special study.[89] The material is considerable and scattered, but full of interest. In the Borough of Lambeth Archives Department (formerly the Minet Library) is a MS programme book for the years 1790 and 1791 in which it is possible to trace the songs sung at Vauxhall through two complete seasons.[90] The MS prompt book for the Master of Ceremonies for the following year, 1792, is in the Theater Collection at Harvard University; it is annotated with lively comments on the musical performances. Such archives also hold huge amounts of music of individual hits as well as collections like this. Another compendium, *Words of the Principal Songs, Rondeaus, Glees performed this evening at Vauxhall Gardens*, was published by E. Spragg and 'sold at the gardens', an obvious form of souvenir: one such copy is annotated with a note that identifies the evening as 9th July 1801.[91]

Between 1790 and 1820 there was a stream of famous singers appearing at the Gardens: Mrs Franklin, Mrs Martyr, Mrs Mountain, Mrs Bland, and the great Mrs Billington, daughter of the Mrs Weischell who is singing in Rowlandson's drawing (slide 23). Among the male singers were Darley, Mountain, Denman, and the boy soprano Welsh. Anna Storace, sister of the composer of Vauxhall and Marylebone songs, and Miss Tyrer – respectively Neapolitan and Irish – were singers in the Gardens, but also made appearances in ballad operas and burlesques in the regular theatres. Later still such *artistes* appeared as Catherine Tinstall, Miss Love, Mr Templeton and Mme Vestris – famous for her rendition of 'Cherry Ripe'. They were all part of a two-way traffic between the seasonal garden-theatre trade and the regular theatre work of the capital. Some published collections of songs were specifically associated with individual singers, like J. C. Bach's *A Second Collection of Favourite Songs Sung at Vaux Hall by Mrs Pinto and Mrs Weischell.*

Between Tyers's opening of the Gardens and the end of the eighteenth century the range of music offered at Vauxhall increased hugely. At first there was only instrumental music, but an aria from Handel's *Acis and Galatea* features on a programme of 1739 and thereafter the vocal contributions were substantial. Thomas Arne, the accredited composer for Vauxhall from 1745, made his settings of Shakespeare songs especially for the Gardens. The basically pastoral ballad fare of the earlier years was elaborated by introducing elements of Italianate opera; choruses from oratorios like Handel's *Saul* were offered when large forces were available. According to Grove, less of the instrumental music was specifically composed for these garden-theatres and less came from English composers. Orchestras were of between twenty and twenty-four players. Organs, perhaps because they required a single player, were popular with managements: Vauxhall's was installed in 1737, Ranelagh's in 1746. Burney played on the latter, as did the young Mozart in 1764. Band performances were also popular: Handel's *Music for the Royal Fireworks*, performed on 21 April 1749, was among the earliest; while by 1790 and until 1816 Vauxhall had the services of the band of the Coldstream Guards.

Composers, singers, instrumentalists and other musicians could appear at various garden-theatres, even though managements liked to preserve an 'exclusive' right to any popular figure. This movement of performers marks a convenient moment for looking at Ranelagh, Vauxhall's chief rival, as well as at some other garden-theatres.

D   **RANELAGH, AND SOME OTHER GARDEN THEATRES, RIVALS TO VAUXHALL**

28   **A view of the canal, Chinese building, Rotunda, in Ranelagh Gardens, with masquerade, etc.**
               (Coloured engraving. 1750s. Guildhall Library.)
29   **The inside view of the Rotunda, Ranelagh Gardens with the company at breakfast**
               (Coloured engraving, 1750s. Guildhall Library.)
30   **The jubilee ball after the Venetian manner**
               (Engraving, 1749. Guildhall Library.)

Ranelagh House and Gardens were first opened on 5 April 1742, with a public breakfast. Within three weeks Horace Walpole had reported to a correspondent: 'I have been breakfasting this morning at Ranelagh Gardens: they have built an immense amphitheatre with balconies full of little ale-houses: it is in rivalry to Vauxhall and cost above twelve thousand pounds'.[92] The amphitheatre (later called the Rotunda) had been specially constructed in the grounds of the Earl of Ranelagh's former house in Chelsea, to the east of the hospital and beside the Thames. This house still stood and was used for Ranelagh's entertainments.

The architect of the Rotunda was William Jones and his (largely wooden) creation was 555 feet in circumference with an internal diameter of 150 feet. Inside, though occasionally compared with the Pantheon in Rome,[93] it resembled nothing more than a circular theatre with a ring of supper boxes, numbering fifty-two in the early 1790s, surmounted with another circle of boxes which were entered from the gallery that ran round the outside of the building. In the centre of this vast building was a 'grand and elegant structure' which in fact contained a chimney and an open fire. In the first instance it had accommodated an orchestra, so that the boxes all gave upon this focal point; but for acoustic reasons it was moved to the side, with the organ behind, as can be seen in slide 29, so that the boxes now gave on to the social area of the floor, achieving the same effect as the exedras of supper booths at Vauxhall. The romantic Lydia Melford in *Humphry Clinker* was entranced:

> Ranelagh looks like the enchanted palace of a genie, adorned with the most exquisite performances of painting, carving, and gilding, enlightened with a thousand golden lamps that emulate the noonday sun; crowded with the great, the rich, the gay, the happy and the fair; glittering with cloth of gold and silver, lace, embroidery, and precious stones. While these exulting sons and daughters of felicity tread this round of pleasure, or regale in different parties, and separate lodges, with fine imperial tea and other delicious refreshments, their ears are entertained with the most ravishing delights of music, both instrumental and vocal.[94]

The grounds proved equally charming. At the end of the seventeenth century the gardens of Ranelagh had been 'curiously kept and elegantly designed', and it is obvious that some of this must have survived when the gardens were opened to the public. The *Description* of 1762 gives considerable space to them: folding doors at the rear of the supper boxes gave into the gardens which were crossed by gravel paths. At the back of the Rotunda was an octagonal grass plot on the far side of which were two 'thatched hovels painted white, formed by four arches and terminating at the top in a point'; these contributed 'a beautiful simplicity' which must 'sensibly affect every spectator with a strong idea of rural pleasures and amusements'. The rivalry with Vauxhall's noted country aspect shows itself clearly there. There were serpentine walks, a circular Temple of Pan on a mound, and the so-called Chinese Temple on the canal (this is depicted in slide 28). Where the canal reached the river there was some sort of grotto, while between the Rotunda and Ranelagh House sometime before 1762 was a flower garden surrounded by shady walks. The *Description* ends with a brief disquisition upon the Chinese art of laying out grounds, which had always been associated with the English informal manner and which the presence of the quasi-Chinese temple on the canal had doubtless suggested.

The competition between Ranelagh and Vauxhall was intense. It is probably no accident, as Brian Allen has pointed out,[95] that Hayman's pictures at Vauxhall were unveiled at about the time Ranelagh opened on the opposite bank of the Thames. It was a matter of constant social moment to decide which Gardens were the better: Walpole and Lord Chesterfield opted strongly for Ranelagh;[96] in Garrick's *High Life Below Stairs* one maid affects to prefer Vauxhall, the other, Ranelagh, while in the same writer's

Epilogue to Murphy's *All in the Wrong* (1761) the food at each is compared:

> At Ranelagh – fine rolls and butter see!
> Signior Tenducci, and the best green tea –
> Italian singing is as light as feather,
> Beard is too loud, too powerful for this weather.
> Vauxhall more solidly regales your palates,
> Good wine, cantatas, cold boil'd beef and ballads.

But as the lines remind us it was for more than the food that either of the Gardens would be in the public eye. Managements vied with each other to provide entertainment that eclipsed their rival's. A brief sketch of this can be offered here.

As slide 30 makes clear, masquerades were a prominent feature of Ranelagh. This famous one took place on Wednesday 26 April 1749 'in the Venetian taste', though Walpole said it had nothing Venetian about it. Nevertheless, it was 'the best understood and prettiest spectacle I ever saw', and he describes it at length:

> It began at three o'clock; at about five, people of fashion began to go; when you entered, you found the whole garden filled with masks and spread with tents, which remained all night very commodely. In one quarter was a May-pole dressed with garlands, and people dancing round it to a tabor and pipe, and rustic music, all masked, as were all the various bands of music that were disposed in different parts of the garden; some like huntsmen with French-horns, some like peasants, and a troop of harlequins and scaramouches in the little open temple on the mount. On the canal was a sort of gondola, adorned with flags and streamers, and filled with music, rowing about. All round the outside of the amphitheatre were shops, filled with Dresden china, Japan, &c., and all the shopkeepers in mask. The amphitheatre was illuminated, and in the middle was a circular bower, composed of all kinds of firs in tubs, from twenty to thirty feet high; under them, orange trees, with small lamps in each orange, and below them all sorts of the finest auriculas in pots; and festoons of natural flowers hanging from tree to tree. Between the arches, too, were firs, and smaller ones in the balconies above. There were booths for tea and wine, gaming-tables, and dancing, and about two thousand persons. In short, it pleased me more than the finest thing I ever saw.[97]

As Walpole's account implies, Ranelagh seems always to have been or been considered more fashionable than Vauxhall, a place with more *ton*. Complaints against the intrusion of riff-raff were made of both gardens, but those voiced for Ranelagh are the more outraged. A music licence for the mornings was withheld by the magistrates in 1754 and the musical breakfasts were discontinued. The Gardens were otherwise opened on Monday, Wednesday and Friday evenings. In the intervals of the concerts the company promenaded through the gardens, a spectacle that was for many the prime entertainment.

Musical fare was substantially the same as at Vauxhall. Singers like Guilia Frasi appeared in 1751 and 1752; Parry, the blind Welsh harper, a few years earlier.

Ferdinando Tenducci, the castrato mentioned in Garrick's lines quoted above, was one of many performers from the regular theatre; he appeared in opera at Dublin and Edinburgh as well as London. Michael Kelly, who had sung in the first performance of *Figaro* in Vienna sang at Ranelagh Gardens in 1782 in Giardini's oratorio *Ruth*. The great tenor Charles Incledon who sang at Covent Garden from the 1790s till 1815 performed at both Ranelagh and Vauxhall. 'An entertainment by actors from Covent Garden' was specifically announced on a handbill for February 1791, while Charles Dibdin produced his 'new Musical Entertainment, in the manner of the Italian Comic Serenatas' for the Jubilee Ridotto at Ranelagh in May 1769. It was *The Ephesian Matron*, with words by Bickerstaffe, and it was popular enough to be repeated several times as part of the usual evening concerts (it lasted an hour); it was also presented at the Little Haymarket Theatre at the end of that August.

Choruses from oratorios, burlesque odes, catches, glees with instrumental parts by Arne, music by Handel and Haydn, orchestral scores employing (for the Regatta Ball of 1775) 240 musicians – these were the programme for the Ranelagh evenings. When the eight-and-a-half year-old Mozart played some of his own compositions for harpsichord and organ during the summer of 1764, the event gave 'the highest Pleasure, Delight and Surprise to the greatest Judges of Music in England or Italy'.[98]

Fireworks became a prominent attraction after 1767, and they remained one of Ranelagh's 'specialities' until it closed. In 1797 the images created with fireworks included two rattlesnakes in pursuit of a butterfly.[99] Huge transparencies were displayed in a building in the grounds, obviously in emulation of those in the walks at Vauxhall. Then there was the famous Mount Ætna, first seen in May 1792, with scenes by Marinari who was 'painter to the Opera'. The idea was presumably derived from the Forge of Vulcan presented by Torré, the fireworks master, in Marylebone Gardens some twenty years before (see next slide). The Ranelagh piece showed Mount Ætna and the Cavern of Vulcan with the Cyclops forging the armour of Mars 'as described in the Aeneid of Virgil'. Accompanied by music from Gluck, Haydn, Giardini and Handel, the smoke was seen to thicken, 'the crater on the top of Etna vomits forth flames, and the lava rolls dreadful along the side of the mountain. This continued with increasing violence till there is a prodigious eruption, which finished with a tremendous explosion'.[100] Such shows were, as Altick has described, a feature of the London entertainment world by the beginning of the nineteenth century; Ranelagh as well as Vauxhall, which continued much further into the century than its rival and therefore displays this aspect of its theatre history more prominently, came to function as a combination of concert hall, circus – there were fencing matches, diving displays – hall of varieties, educational exhibition hall and light opera house. We shall explore this eclectic function and repertoire further when we turn to Vauxhall's history during the first half of the nineteenth century (slides 36–50). The last entertainments took place at Ranelagh on 8 July 1803; two years later the House and the Rotunda were demolished.

31   View of the orchestra with the band of music, the Grand Walk, &c. in Marylebone Gardens
(Etching and engraving, hand-coloured, published by R. Sayer and T. Bennett, after 1750. Yale Center for British Art, New Haven, Connecticut.)

Like both Vauxhall and Ranelagh, Marylebone had its origin in an earlier garden. But it was effectively opened in 1738 by Daniel Gough, the proprietor of the Rose of Normandy, a tavern on the High Street through which the earlier gardens and their bowling-greens were approached. Before 1738 there had been occasional entertainments: in 1718 some illuminations, a musical concert on the King's birthday and in 1736 a Flying Man who flew down on a rope from scaffolding 135 feet high pushing a wheelbarrow before him.[101]

Under the management of Mr. Gough a band drawn from the Opera and theatres played during the evenings in a garden-orchestra obviously modelled on that at Vauxhall. There were balls, suppers and public breakfasts. Under Gough's successor the gardens were expanded and improved, and – despite the dangerous area in which they were situated – they acquired the reputation of being the largest and politest such assembly place in London. Among its claims to theatrical fame is the performance there in 1758 of *La Serva Padrona*, adapted from Pergolesi by the elder Storace and the proprietor's son, Trusler, who later became a clergyman. In these earlier years there were only occasional firework displays and masquerades.

In 1763 the Gardens were leased by the tenor, Thomas ('Tommy') Lowe, who had performed at Vauxhall to great applause. At Marylebone he presented concerts with a variety of singers, but in which he himself took a prominent part. In 1765 Dr Boyce's song 'Solomon' was sung as well as Handel's 'Let the merry bells go round', in which Mrs Vincent was accompanied by a new instrument known as the Tintinnabula. Lowe's management ran into difficulties, and his creditors continued to run the Gardens while he himself took work at Finch's Grotto (for which see slide 32).

The last ten years of Marylebone Gardens, ending with its developing into streets and houses in 1778, were much the same as before. The musician, Samuel Arnold, ran them with verve and some enlargement of the programmes. Fireworks by Torré were especially popular from 1772 to 1774. Singers and musicians and composers and librettists were engaged in profusion, but in the end Marylebone seems to have been unable to compete with Vauxhall and Ranelagh, its principal rivals.

32   Map of the garden-theatres on the south bank of the Thames
(From W. S. Scott, Green Retreats, p.114, using modern street names.)

During the eighteenth century there were many small establishments modelled on the pattern of Vauxhall or Ranelagh or Marylebone but without their scope or sophistication. As this map shows, many were clustered in the area just north of Vauxhall itself. The remainder were focused around taverns, tea rooms, or springs (Lambeth Wells, Finch's Grotto, Restoration Spring Gardens), their staple offerings being music and dancing. The enterprising proprietor of Cumberland Gardens opened early to catch people on their way to nearby Vauxhall. Cumberland too, tried to ape the other more fashionable gardens with a *Fête Champêtre* in 1779 and a Ranelagh-like sailing contest for which a silver cup was offered in 1796.[102] As soon as they seemed to be prospering these gardens would extend their premises with a 'Great Room', as at Lambeth Wells or The Dog and Duck, the latter with an organ. The Dog and Duck seems to have exercised the most ingenuity in attracting customers away from its rivals: a bowling-green was succeeded by a swimming pool in 1769, 200 feet long by almost 100 wide. Few were able to put themselves on the musical map, though under Ireland Lambeth Wells formed its own society which met once a month under the direction of a neighbouring church organist.

Most of these small gardens sprang up in the wake of Vauxhall and withered sooner or later. Marble Hall had the longest life from 1740 until 1813. Most perished when magistrates refused to renew their licences (Lambeth Wells, The Dog and Duck). The Restoration Spring Gardens were let in 1771 to William Curtis, the famous botanist and author of *Flora Londinensis* (1775–1798), and for nearly twenty years he admitted subscribers to the botanical garden he created there. Other metamorphoses were more extreme: the Great Room of Lambeth Spa was leased to a Methodist congregation to use for their services. Nevertheless, the mushrooming of these south-bank pleasure resorts testifies to the strong appeal of especially musical *venues* to a metropolitan clientele who enjoyed going to the 'theatre' in a garden. Two further gardens marked on this map are discussed in the next two slides: Cuper's and the Temple of Apollo.

33 Entrance to Cuper's Gardens
(Watercolour. Guildhall Library. p.LI/CUP.)

Opened in 1690 or 1691 by Boydell Cuper, these were rather like Vauxhall – favoured with pleasantly laid-out walks, arbours and a distinctly garden 'feel' which the popular song recorded:

> 'Twas down in Cupid's Garden
> For pleasure I did go
> To see the fairest flowers
> That in the garden grow.

As the line shows, it was also known as Cupid's Gardens, and marked as such on eighteenth-century maps. Whether for its popularity with city lovers or on account of some statue of Cupid among the sculpture acquired by Cuper from the famous collection of marbles from Arundel House on the other side of the Thames is not clear.[103]

In 1738 the Gardens were taken by Ephraim Evans, a taverner from Fleet Street, who improved the facilities and constructed an orchestra with an organ. His widow ran them even more effectively, providing good music and elaborate fireworks: in 1741 she offered the fire music from Handel's *Atalanta* and two years later a display which represented Medusa's snaky head. In virtually its last season the fireworks building contained a perspective view of Rhodes – the sea, city, buildings, landscape, a model of the Colossus, dolphins, a moving Neptune, waterworks and fireworks.

As a result of the new law of 1752 controlling places of public entertainment, Cuper's or Cupid's was refused a licence the following year. Mrs Evans changed their function into a Tea Gardens, and two years later used the device of being open only to subscribers to evade the terms of the act and revive the evening entertainments. But its fortunes had waned and the last recorded event there was a private concert in August 1759. The gardens which Johnson had visited[104] first became part of a wine and vinegar firm and then were absorbed into the approaches to the new Waterloo Bridge.

34   **Orchestra room of the Apollo Gardens**
           (Watercolour in grangerized Public Gardens of London, *collected and arranged by John Fillingham. Guildhall Museum.)*

If Cuper's Gardens is an example of a late seventeenth-century garden like the New Spring Gardens, which grew into a place of entertainment by the middle of the next century, as the Spring Gardens became Vauxhall, the Apollo Gardens is an instance of one which flourished late in the eighteenth century. It was open between 1789 and 1793.

Sometimes known as the Temple of Apollo, its principal feature was the concert room (with organ) capable of holding over 1,000 people and a band of seventy musicians. It was decorated with paintings of a moon (in a kind of orrery in the dome); further paintings of Don Quixote were on the walls of garden arbours. The vista shown on this slide is presumably the 'curious scene, painted in a pleasing manner, which concealed the orchestra from the public view';[105] what it also seems to present is a trompe l'oeil of a garden seen from inside the concert room. Although (or perhaps because) the proprietor boasted of the patronage of the well-to-do who came to enjoy 'the superior excellence of the Music and Wines', Apollo Gardens became notorious for pickpockets and was closed by the magistrates about 1793.

In 1790 it was called a 'Petit-Vauxhall',[106] which suggests the fashion in which the success of the original Vauxhall Gardens came to be imitated, not only in England but (as the next slide will show) abroad as well. The orchestra was removed from The Temple of Apollo and erected in Sydney Gardens, Bath; a watercolour plan of this hexagonal square in Bath, now in the Guildhall Library, London, marks the gardens there as 'Sidney Garden Vauxhall'.[107]

35   **Interior view of a Vauxhall**
           (French school, second half of 18th century. Pen and ink. Musée Carnavalet, Paris. H.O., 279; W.O., 762.)

As the commentary upon the last slide began to suggest, the influence of Vauxhall was enormous. Its special combination of garden and theatre was frequently imitated, and its name became synonymous with open air amusements. Thus Horace Walpole on a visit to Stowe in Buckinghamshire reported that 'A small Vauxhall was acted for us at the Grotto in the Elysian Fields, which was illuminated with lamps, as were the thickets and two little banks on the lake'.[108] There was a Vauxhall at Duddlestone Hall, near Birmingham, in 1758, and a Ranelagh at Passy, near Paris.[109] When Carl Philipp Moritz came to the London Vauxhall in 1782 it struck him as having 'some resemblance to our Berlin Vauxhall'.[110] The word for a station in Russian (vokzal) commemorates a Vauxhall at a terminus of the Petersburg–Pavlovsk line in 1837. The Tivoli founded in Copenhagen in 1843 was yet another Vauxhall imitation, though this time it took its name from the famous Italian villa at Tivoli (one of the many Italian sources noted earlier in this discussion for London's garden-theatres).

Many European capitals seem to have imitated and borrowed the name of Vauxhall: there were examples in the Hague and – this slide – in Paris. There were, in fact, several places of entertainment which acquired the generic name of a Vauxhall during the eighteenth century.[111] They were used for balls, receptions, concerts, various shows and for painting exhibitions. Many of them were temporary establishments. It has been suggested that this drawing, unless it is simply a project, records the first 'Vauxhall' created in 1766 just off the Boulevard Saint-Martin by the firework maker Torré, who later demonstrated his skills at Ranelagh. It was a rectangular hall with a rotunda, open-sided, in the middle, as can faintly be seen here; the fireworks on the table to the right of the scene were an invention of Dominique Dupuis.[112]

E   **VAUXHALL IN THE NINETEENTH CENTURY**

36   **The Romp, or the Great Catalani: sung with unprecedented applause by Miss Feron**
(Copper engraving, 1809, published by Laurie and Whittle. Robert Douwma (Prints and Maps) Ltd.)

37   **Mock battle**
(Etching and aquatint, about 1815. Yale Center for British Art, New Haven, Connecticut. B1977.14.18712.)

38   **Stage with acrobats in Vauxhall Gardens**
(Etching. Guildhall Library.)

Vauxhall's entertainments in the nineteenth century were a continuation of its successes from the previous decades, but elaborated and varied in ever more ingenious ways. A commentary of 1837 gave as its opinion that 'To analyze the entertainments at Vauxhall would be about as easy as to fix the outlines of smoke. Everything is so evanescent, so intangible, and so like a vision, that it is scarcely possible to assign a distinct character to any part of the agreeable varieties with which the gardens abound'.[113] A playbill for Monday 19 September 1842 calls Vauxhall 'This mirror of public amusements'[114]; indeed, it seemed to reflect the whole gamut of popular entertainments that were available in London. The richness of its programmes combined with – and partly caused by – the management's need to go ever one better than their last show is recorded in dozens of playbills in archives in London (the British Library, Guildhall Library), Oxford (the Bodley) and Harvard (Theater Collection). From this vast deposit of information have been selected items which will allow the history of this extraordinary *venue* to be sketched. Even so, it is hard to fix the outlines of smoke.

These first three slides indicate Vauxhall's range of entertainment. Songs and musical concerts continued, but the public craved more and more spectacular shows. Managements responded with elaborate circus acts or huge representations of battles and cities, made all the more unusual by their open-air setting. Some list of 'firsts' will suggest the managements' inventiveness. In 1802 were introduced the Pandean Minstrels who performed continental airs after the main concert: each of the five players used a set of pipes fastened around his neck as well as either the cymbals, triangle, bells, tambourine or drum at the same time. The same year saw the first appearance of a fire-balloon in which Mr Garnerin ascended from the Gardens; Southworth quotes a contemporary account:

> At twelve two guns were fired; and a lighted lamp having been affixed to the slack of the rope, it was cut adrift and ascended most majestically and gradually. When it got just above the high trees it appeared to be in an eddy of wind, and was declining. It presently, however, cleared off, and ascended very fast and high. In about six minutes the lower valve burst and emitted considerable flames, but soon they subsided. A second broke, which had still greater effect; and so on a third containing rockets went off with a greater explosion. The whole was highly applauded and succeeded by M. Ruggieri's fireworks which we cannot but say were inimitable for beauty, variety and effect.[115]

Mme Garnerin also made an ascent two weeks later, reaching a height of 600 feet and landing safely between Primrose Hill and Hampstead. On another occasion a cat descended on a parachute. Such ballooning events were ever popular and we shall encounter more of them in connection with later slides. In 1815 marionettes were presented in a crescent near the Rotunda; in 1818, Mlle Lefort, the original 'bearded lady', and the resourceful and popular Mme Saqui, the tight-rope walker. She, her husband and child executed marvellous feats of dancing on the ropes, but the most acclaimed of her acts was her descent from the top of a mast sixty feet high through the fire and smoke of the habitual firework display. Again, a contemporary reaction from the *Literary Gazette* is worth quoting:

> A human figure, moving in a burning atmosphere and at so great a height from 'solid earth' presents a most imposing spectacle. For ourselves we can only say that it rivals what our imagination has conjured up from the enchantments of the Arabian Nights. This surprising female sparkling with spangles and tinsel and her head canopied with plumes of ostrich feathers ascends the rope to a man seated at the top in the midst of blue lights and a hundred wheels and stars and rockets; thence she again descends with a rapid step, stopping only for a few moments near the center of the long and dazzling line.[116]

Her salary of 100 guineas a week obviously reflected her drawing powers. She owned her own theatre in Paris.

In 1825 professional dancers, under the direction of M. Hullin of the Royal Academy of Music in Paris, were introduced; their ballets were diversified with dialogue, songs and imitations. These dancers were part of efforts by a new management, Messrs Bish and Gye, who had bought the Gardens in 1821 from the last descendent of the Tyers family, to refurbish Vauxhall.[117] Among their more important innovations was the construction of a ballet theatre in the Cross Walk. Its stage was fifty feet high, forty wide and had a depth of four wings. The scenery was beautifully painted by the younger Thorn, Meyrick, Morris and Hollogan; the drop curtain displayed a view of Lake Albano, one of the great picturesque sites on the contemporary Grand Tour. This stage can be seen in use in slide 38. Another, smaller stage was created inside the Rotunda where the old orchestra had stood (see slide 39).

Vauxhall was, in fact, becoming more theatrical than musical. Performances – whether tight-rope walkers, dancers, marionettes, balloon ascents – were featured in ways that increasingly had the aspect of the conventional theatre: prosceniums, wings, scenery, effects and with the audience allotted seats or at least a viewing station (as in slide 47). This stabilizing of Vauxhall's theatre can be best seen in the history of its representations of battles (see slide 37).

Naumachias or representations of sea fights had been a feature of ancient Roman theatre; we know that the Colosseum was able to stage them with real water and miniature ships. They were imitated, too, in the fountains and hydraulic theatres of Italian Renaissance gardens. So it was perhaps almost inevitable that Vauxhall should have opted for *naumachia*. In 1814 the space at the end of the Grand Walk was converted into a scene for engagements at sea, though in the absence of water the effects were created by sound, the inevitable fireworks and painted representations of ships which cruised about, caught fire and generally executed various maritime manoeuvres. Not the least of Vauxhall's ambitions was to compete with the regular theatres where such exploits were presented with more technical assistance, like the Siege of Gibraltar shown in 1812 at the Sadler's Wells water tank.

In 1827 Vauxhall Gardens mounted its most ambitious and extravagant battle, this time 'on land'. The two-hour Battle of Waterloo was staged in an open-air theatre which accommodated 1,200 spectators and was constructed in front of the fireworks tower at the far end of the Italian Walk. This was Vauxhall's challenge to the Waterloo presented at Astley's Amphitheatre three years earlier, and it was arranged by Farley of the Theatre Royal, Covent Garden. The advertisement ran, in part, as follows:

> In this GRAND SPECTACLE, upwards of
> 1000 SOLDIERS; HORSE AND FOOT, WILL BE ENGAGED; and Mr COOKE, From the
> Royal Amphitheatre, Liverpool, will bring into action his unrivalled STUD OF
> HORSES, with numerous auxiliaries, aided by the use of Artillery,
> Ammunition Wagons, &c. &c. THE ACTION is to form an exact
> Representation of the Field of Battle, with the various Buildings of the Farm
> houses, La Belle Alliance, Hougoumont, &c. &c., which are erected in the
> same relative situations as on the plains of Waterloo, viz. La Belle Alliance
> was on the right of the centre of the British Line; and in the rear of their left
> was a small Wood; and the opportunities which the grounds Vauxhall
> afford of realizing this situation, no stage or gardens in Europe can equal.
> The action commenced by Bonaparte ordering the troops on the left to

attack the Wood and Chateau of Gomont. The assault was most furious and sanguinary; the walls surrounding the Gardens of Hougoumont were loop-holed by the British Troops, and every means of defence adopted. During the struggle the French Cavalry made a desperate rush to surround the Duke of Wellington, but was prevented by a quick movement of our troops, who encompassed him by forming a diamond square that baffled all their attempts. At this time, the French line is making a quick movement through the wood, on the left, and from the right of the Hill, the Prussian Flag is seen waving; the troops of Bulow cover the British, and their United Forces put the French to the rout.

A GENERAL ATTACK OF CAVALRY AND INFANTRY

is made upon them; the enemy is forced to retreat in disorder; and the whole becomes a complete scene of havoc and slaughter, during which various accidents occur; in particular that of

AN AMMUNITION WAGGON BLOWING UP!

Which is drawn all over the Field, in Flames, by the terrified Horses. —Buonaparte, seeing all his efforts to recover his lost ground ineffectual, and his whole Array in confusion, betakes himself to his Chariot, and is seen driving across the Field, pursued by the British Cavalry. Whole heaps of Men and Horses lay expiring on the ensanguined Plain.

THE CHATEAU OF GOMONT IN FLAMES!

All forming a Terrific but Glorious Picture of the memorable 18th of June.[118]

It was far too expensive an event to repeat, although what must have been a cheaper version was seen by Charles Dickens on 29 June 1849; that was a time when Vauxhall was fighting to keep its head above water and when famous items from its past repertoire were revived in some form or other.[119] But the location created for the original spectacle in 1827, with its special stage and 'auditorium', was utilized for other shows, the most grandiose of which was the 1834 representation of Captain Ross's arctic expedition, with wooden icebergs and 70 foot high scenery.

39   **Ring and stage inside the Vauxhall Rotunda**
(J. Findlay. Watercolour, 1859. The Museum of London.)

This is one of a series of watercolours by Findlay in the Museum of London which depict the actual dismantling of Vauxhall Gardens. They constitute a most important record which deserves to be better known. The artist is presumably J. Findlay, who was active around 1825 to the late 1850s and specialized in topographical views. There are just over forty watercolours by him in the British Museum Print Room, one of them showing the entrance to Vauxhall Gardens.

This series from which our slide is taken (another is slide 50) gives various interior views of the buildings as the draperies and pictures are being dismantled; to the left of this drawing workmen are removing some screen or door. But a view of the small stage and circus ring in the Rotunda is shown at this stage in the history of the Gardens to establish some further aspects of its various theatrical repertoire.

The Rotunda had, of course, often been revamped. In 1789 it became a 'superb Eastern Tent'; in 1802, a Pavilion of Concord. The small theatre and ring were part of the refurbishments carried out by the new management that took over in 1821. Both were a response to the challenges from other London entertainments and to the need to have some scope for the amusement of clients in bad weather, since Vauxhall had always been especially susceptible to the vagaries of English summers. There were, of course, other circus rings in the metropolis, but this allowed Vauxhall to mount its own displays of equestrian skills.[120] It was also a flexible arrangement, for in 1848 Van Amburgh exhibited his wild animals on the stage of the Rotunda with the audience placed in the ring after the horsemanship was finished. These two – stage and arena – afforded Vauxhall even more versatility than the various locations in the gardens themselves.

40   C. H. Simpson, ESQ' MCRGV
(Etching by W. Kidd after Robert Cruikshank. 20 August 1833. Guildhall Library.)

On 19 April 1833 a special Benefit Night at the Gardens celebrated the retirement after thirty-six years of its famous master of ceremonies, C. H. Simpson. Robert Cruikshank drew the scene, which was published (this slide) the following day with this inscription:

> For upwards of 36 years – with a distant view of his Colossal Likeness in Varigated Lamps. To C. H. Simpson Esq: M.C. of the Royal Gardens Vauxhall this print taken in the sixty-third year of his age on the Night of his benefit is, by express permission most respectfully dedicated by his obliged and humble servant – the Publisher.

The Gardens outdid themselves to make their farewell to a man who had devoted himself with panache and a suitable love of artifice to promoting the delights of Vauxhall. The programme included a transparency of Antwerp; a water scene representing the Triumph of Britannia, complete with water rockets; the military brass band of His Highness the Grand Duke of Darmstadt; and, above all, a huge, illuminated silhouette of the unforgettable figure of the MCRGV – Master of Ceremonies Royal Garden Vauxhall (Vauxhall became Royal in 1822 under the patronage of George IV). This image showed Simpson in his habitual *tenue* of silk stockings, knee breeches, cutaway coat, and silver-headed cane as rod of office.

But the 'Colossal' likeness and the flowery prose of the published picture capture the Simpson effect; even the quasi-regal dedication ('by express permission . . .') identifies part of his calculated act. It is unclear whether the dedication and its wording hint at some satire – probably not, for Simpson himself was quite without a sense of humour and, as the Gardens' publicist since just before the turn of the century, had conducted himself with a solemnity that was aptly endorsed by the elaboration of his famous prose style. He possessed a somewhat effeminate voice, with mannered emphases and phrasing; he was skilled in celebrating with fulsome compliment every aspect of the kingdom, the metropolis and the Gardens, and (in Southworth's happy phrase) he 'threaded the maze of verbosity to the subject matter' of each speech.[121]

Simpson certainly epitomized a crucial element of Vauxhall. Dandified, good natured, with an incurable air of *politesse* (bows and genuflections directed towards his clients) and an uncritical love of showmanship, he saw Vauxhall struggling to maintain its reputation with visitors. Ever greater and greater efforts were made to put the Gardens in the public eye, as the next sequence of slides indicates. What Simpson strikingly represented was, on the one hand, gentility: with his dandified clothes and manners he symbolized the ideal Vauxhall patron. Yet, on the other hand, especially as the nineteenth century advanced, he was an exotic reminder of old times, a memento of days of elegance and suavity which it was the business of Vauxhall's managers to persuade their clients could still be experienced south of the Thames. However, such sentimental recollections of earlier days were not by themselves able to sustain Vauxhall's fortunes. Exoticism of a stronger kind was needed; more attention to the scientific and to the adventurous began to mingle with the standard items of music and vaudeville and circus.

41   **Vauxhall Gardens poster for 14 August 1826**
     (Johnson Collection, The Bodleian Library. G. A. Surrey C.23.)
42   **Vauxhall Gardens poster for 11 August [1834]**
     (Johnson Collection, The Bodleian Library (London Play Places 6).)
43   **Vauxhall Gardens handbill for 19 July 1838**
     (From a grangerized History of Vauxhall Gardens (1890), V, 53 (left).
     Harvard University Theater Collection.)
44   **Double poster for 4 and 7 October [?1840]**
     (Guildhall Library. C.27.)
45   **Vauxhall Gardens handbill for 1842**
     (From a grangerized History of Vauxhall Gardens (1890), VII, 21. Harvard
     University Theater Collection.)

These posters from the years 1826 to 1842 suggest the kind of entertainments by which Vauxhall Gardens sought to attract and keep its customers. Programmes contrived a variety of items ('stage novelties'[122]) so that all tastes might be satisfied in the course of an evening. The staple ingredients of a Vauxhall evening were: fireworks;[123] balloon ascents, of which more later; displays of acrobats and walkers upon the tight-rope and the slack-rope – as can be seen on slide 41 'Mr Blackmore will exhibit his usual Evolutions on . . .'; ballet; Italian opera; stars from the regular theatre – Mlle Grisi of the King's Theatre (slide 42); a range of circus acts, but notably riding – in slide 45 Mlle Caroline, who arrived that summer with her display of horses from Paris, is billed; the endless panoramas of edifying or picturesque subjects – Mt Blanc, one hundred feet in length, was hugely popular, but slide 43 gives a characteristically rich set of painted views; military bands. The invention and much of the effect of the posters and handbills was to convey the sense of a dizzy and never-ending succession of acts and entertainments. Closer scrutiny reveals that ingenious wording and alteration of typefaces contrived more variety and changes than were, in practice, possible; it is the *illusion* of Vauxhall's inexhaustible magic that was promoted, while the actual repertoire continued to rely upon a dozen basic items. For the Queen's Birthday in 1833 'An entire change of entertainments' was announced: 'the Proprietors (it was claimed) have, in every department, made unparalleled exertions to produce Novelty and effect in each'. Yet they are the same old items.[124]

Plays and songs were still announced as 'written expressly' for Vauxhall,[125] though clearly *artistes* from other venues and theatres appeared in the Gardens without fresh material: such as Ching Lauro, a posture master familiar in pantomimes, or Ducrow's horses or Ramo Samee, the Indian juggler and sword-swallower. When 'Professor Keller' arrived in London to present his corps of male and female posturists *(Poses Plastiques and Grands Tableaux Vivants)* Vauxhall was one of half a dozen places where he performed.[126] He was said to be a teacher of gymnastics at the University of Berlin. One of the much promoted items at Vauxhall which did offer unique opportunities for its visitors and yet drew upon the talents of personnel associated with the regular theatre was the painted scenes. Artists like Thomas Stothard and Clarkson Stanfield who were scene designers and painters (the latter considered by John Ruskin to be second only to Turner) provided pictures: on 21 August 1826 a playbill included 'Ruins of an Italian Abbey Produced by the celebrated Mr. Stanfield'.[127]

As some of these items begin to suggest, two recurring emphases of the Victorian phase of Vauxhall are exoticism and edification. The famous view of Antwerp is announced as 'a highly finished (almost a Fac Simile) resemblance'[128] obviously in an attempt to emphasize its educational value. There were scientific displays too: of optical science in 1852 while, in 1839–40, Mr H. Carter exhibited his 'New and Extraordinary 'KONIAPHOSTIC' or 'LIME LIGHT', a chemical combination of such vivid brilliancy and diffusiveness, as completely to Illumine the Whole Gardens by One Central Light'.[129] Even varieties from Astleys could be billed at Vauxhall with a quasi-educational air: 'Mr Rochez the Bottle Equilibrast [sic]', while the announcement that 'The Gardens will be emblematically fitted up' gives a spurious weight of high art and learning to some minor revamping of the decor.[130]

Indians had appeared at Vauxhall as early as the 1740s and again in 1762, when Sir Joshua Reynolds painted a portrait of one of the Cherokee chiefs. Indigenous American material seems to have been popular also in the nineteenth century, perhaps because it mixed the exotic and the educational. Catlin's Ojibbeway Indians performed in sundry London locations before arriving at Vauxhall, where against a background of wigwams they demonstrated their horsemanship. In 1848 the negro Juba sang his plantation songs there too.[131]

One method of bringing fresh life to the series of Vauxhall evenings was by announcing special galas, benefit nights or charity openings. Slide 43 announces a Juvenile Fête, and other posters exist for Benefit Nights for Distressed Poles in 1833 when Paganini played,[132] for various *artistes*, and metropolitan and national charities. Special occasions like the coronation of William IV attracted large crowds (40,000 attended on that occasion, doubtless because the Government had financed the opening and no entrance fees were charged on Coronation Day itself).

Fireworks continued to be a central part of Vauxhall's programme – for its Juvenile Fêtes of July 1835 they contrived a picture of a Versailles entertainment under Louis XIV. And when Napoleon III came to the Gardens in 1861 he was greeted with a 'tempest of fireworks'. Like fireworks, ballooning was a unique opportunity to exploit the open-air site and thus present acts with which the traditional theatrical locations could not compete. Balloon ascents started in the early nineteenth century. In 1802 the French aeronaut Garnerin made his debut and the release of a cat in a primitive parachute was an instant success ('Puss in a Parachute'); he also exhibited his night balloon which caught fire. But undoubtedly the most famous ballooning event was the flight by Charles Green in 1836 from the Gardens to Nassau. Leaving at 13.00 hours, he descended at 07.00 hours the following day. The place of his arrival was thereafter used by the management to advertise their 'Nassau Balloon'. The enterprise was acclaimed in the press, in songs and in various verses like these by Barham in the *Ingoldsby Legends*:

> Oh! the balloon, the great balloon,
> It left Vauxhall one Monday at noon,
> And every one said we should hear of it soon
> With news from Aleppo or Scanderoon,
> But very soon after folks changed their tune:
> 'The netting had burst—the silk—the shalloon;—
> It had met with a trade-wind—a deuced monsoon—
> It was blown out to sea—it was blown to the moon—
> They ought to have put off their journey till June;
> Sure none but a donkey, a goose, or baboon
> Would go up in November in any balloon!
>
> Then they talk'd about Green—'Oh! where's Mister Green?
> And where's Mr Holland who hired the machine?
> And where is Monck Mason, the man that has been
> Up so often before—twelve times or thirteen—
> And who writes such nice letters describing the scene?
> And where's the cold fowl, and the ham, and poteen?
> The press'd beef, with the fat cut off—nothing but lean,
> And the portable soup in the patent tureen?
> Have they got to Grand Cairo or reached Aberdeen?
> Or Jerusalem—Hamburg—or Ballyporeen?
> No! they have not been seen! Oh! they haven't been seen! . . . [133]

and so on with the full narrative. Green made a farewell ascent in 1852, and in the meanwhile there had been balloon races, ascents by women, even one projected by a Bengal tiger which did not materialize,[134] excursions with ten people at a time (20 guineas for men, only 10 for women) as well as perhaps the inevitable tragedies. In July 1837 Robert Cocking fell to his death while trying out a new parachute over Kent; a benefit night was held for his widow. In 1847 Albert Smith, having ascended by balloon from Vauxhall Gardens in order to shoot off fireworks over Putney, got caught in a thunderstorm and had to make a forced landing in the Belgrave Road.[135] Smith was a contributor to *Punch*, a writer of fiction and stage pieces, but his ballooning was more of a piece with his stories of an *Ascent of Mt Blanc* or *Overland Mail* and makes clear that the spectators at Vauxhall were eager for the sense of vicarious adventure that these ascents gave them. A manuscript note of receipts in the Harvard Theater Collection shows that ballooning certainly helped the box office: receipts for fourteen nights with ballooning earlier in the day brought in £6,446, while fifty-nine nights when no ballooning had taken place produced only £5,544.[136]

46   The Vauxhall Papers, 1841
         (Bromhead Collection, London University.)

Three times a week between 19 July and 23 August during the season of 1841 the Gardens produced its own magazine, *The Vauxhall Papers*. There were eighteen issues in all.[137] It included advertisements, as on this slide, but it was largely devoted to essays, poems, humorous pieces and – which are especially important for our present purposes – historical accounts of its own past. It also features some charming illustrations by 'Alfred Crowquill'.

It republished John Lockman's letter to Lord Baltimore which has been frequently quoted here; it compared prices in the Gardens between 1774 and 1841; it printed parallel texts of two songs called 'The Pleasures of Vauxhall' – that of 1737 was an easy and generalized pastoral, that of 1841, distinctly popular, jolly, even vulgar. It gave an account of what was even by now the historical ascent of the Nassau Balloon. It described at length Jonathan Tyers's country house garden at Denbies. It carried an article against smoking, which had been forbidden at Vauxhall; written by Alfred Bunn who was then the manager of the Gardens, it castigated 'The habit of Smoking, which has got into such general usage for the last few years in this country', as 'the filthiest a man can contract' (pp.23–24).

The opening shown on this slide, besides a view of crowds listening to the orchestra (the old-fashioned, nostalgic Vauxhall), gives an image by Crowquill of an acrobat, and the start of the description of Denbies. Among the largely equestrian events billed on the left may be seen in the smaller print of the bottom line 'Herr Joel will give his surprising Imitations of Birds'. The employment of this 'Altonian Siffleur' harks back to days when Tyers also paid men to imitate birds in the Vauxhall walks and maintain its country air and reputation.

47   Picture model of Venice in Vauxhall Gardens
         (From Illustrated London News, *12 June 1847. The British Library.)*

This is a late example of one of the most popular and long-established entertainments. There had always been huge transparencies displayed in the gardens at Vauxhall and Ranelagh. In the late eighteenth century these static images had been developed into exciting and elaborate moving pictures: the most famous was the Eidophusikon of Philippe Jacques de Loutherbourg, first performed at his house in Lisle Street on 26

February 1781. He had already established himself as an artist and scene painter, in collaboration with Garrick, at Drury Lane.[138] The Eidophusikon presented extraordinary imitations of natural phenomena – sunrisings, storms, running waters and conflagrations. Its influence upon popular entertainments was immense, and the various transparencies displayed in Vauxhall Gardens had somehow to be able to compete. Its famous 'Cascade', which had entertained eighteenth-century visitors, had used strips of tin to mimic the falls of water. More sophisticated devices were needed to whet the appetites of regular customers.

So it was that the large representations of famous cities – Rhodes, Constantinople, Venice – or of events – the eruptions of Ætna or Vesuvius – became a standard item in these garden-theatres. Once the tin cascade had disappeared in the early nineteenth century, the Saloon offered a contrivance called the Heptaplasiesoptron, whereby glass plates produced reflections of revolving pillars, palm-trees, twining serpents, coloured lamps and a fountain.[139] As often as possible, fireworks were involved with the display of some transparency or painted scenery, as in this show of Venice. These were used with much success between 1823 and 1837 to augment representations of Fingal's Cave, the ruins of an Italian abbey, Virginia Water, the burning of York Minster and of the Houses of Parliament, Mt Blanc, St Michael's Mount and a Balkan pass.

The acrobats and tightrope walkers, whom we have already noticed, contributed the human element. In this view of Venice the acrobat, Joel Il Diavolo, has begun his descent through the smoke and fire; the artist for the *Illustrated London News* has done what other artists before him had done (see slide 7) and aided the illusion by showing Il Diavolo with no visible means of support.

48   **Manners and Customs of Yᵉ Englyshe (New Series) No 9**
(Punch, *July 1850. The British Library.*)

We have come a long way since Rowlandson's picture of company in the Gardens in 1785 and it is time to chronicle the final decline, decay and dissolution of Vauxhall. We have already noted the purchase of the Gardens from the last Tyers descendent in 1821 by Messrs. Bish, Gye and Hughes; they paid £28,000. They reopened the following year with the new title of The Royal Gardens, Vauxhall. Visitors continued to be attracted by the increasingly frantic and shrill advertisements of its varied entertainments, for – as *The Vauxhall Papers* put it – 'That "The Walks are Beautifully varied", of Life itself as well as of Vauxhall Gardens, will admit of little dispute' (p.22). In 1836 the management were desperate enough to open the Gardens during the daytime, with the disappointing results that Charles Dickens recorded in a famous essay in *Sketches by Boz* (see Appendix). Gye went bankrupt in 1840, tried unsuccessfully to sell the Gardens (they were brought in at £20,000), and Vauxhall did not open that year. Some fittings and Hayman pictures were sold at this time. In 1841 they were bought by Thomas Fuller, and under a succession of managers – Bunn, Robert Wardell and Edward Tyrrell Smith – they limped along, not opening at all in 1842 and thereafter for very short seasons and for only a few evenings at a time. Vauxhall was put on the market again in 1845, but no bidder was found. Finances were boosted by the occasional leasing of the Gardens for charity events. The weather proved uncooperative, the gas lighting that was installed in 1846 destroyed the atmosphere, and competition from other theatres and places of entertainment was overpowering. In 1846 Cremorne Gardens opened on a twelve-acre site between Chelsea and Fulham and around its central building which contained a bandstand and dance floor were a 'Chinese pagoda, a Swiss chalet, an Indian temple, a large theatre . . . a marionette theatre, concert room, small circus, restaurant, fernery, menagerie, American bowling saloon, shooting gallery and gypsy's tent'.[140] To add insult to injury, Cremorne acquired the title of Royal in 1857. Vauxhall still struggled to compete with its own bowling saloon and archery ground, with even more lamps and with recurrent advertisements for 'Final' seasons.

It is something of this decline that this *Punch* cartoon captures: the frenzy, the less than genteel clientele, the rather desperate striving for festivity. Doyle's caption in quaint *olde Englyshe* even implies that Vauxhall is entirely a thing of the past. Earlier in 1845 *Punch* had satirized 'sundry ryghte stupidde freakes of ye grosseste humbugge', fun and games belonging to 'Merrie Englande in ye Oldenne Tyme' including an uproariously inexpert archery display, by no means worthy of the modern world.[141] In 1844 a prospectus was issued for the building of the South London Polytechnic Institution on the site; *Punch* satirized this by suggesting that seawater be piped from Margate to turn Vauxhall into one of the new, fashionable seaside resorts.[142] There were still fifteen years of life left in Vauxhall, but it was waning fast; licences were not now so easily obtained because of complaints of rowdiness; in 1855 it did not open at all.

When it did the entertainments were much as before: songs, more balloon ascents, horses, Van Ambrugh's lions, the Cirque Imperial Company (in 1856), Monsieur Leopold's acrobatic troupe, Sam Cowell 'the Muse of Comedy' (in 1858). Here is a programme in full, where the careful puffing (the *enlarged* orchestra, a *limited* number of nights, etc) can be clearly felt:

> The BRASS BAND will play from half-past 7 until 8, Conducted by Mr Bean; Leader, Mr Blight.
>
> At Eight o'Clock precisely—THE GRAND CONCERT, of Vocal and Instrumental Music, will be given in the enlarged Orchestra, under the Direction of Mr ALEXANDER LEE. Principal Vocalists:—Mr Sinclair, his first appearance since his return from America, who is engaged for a limited number of nights; Mr Binge, Mr Hodges, Mr Darcie, Mr J. W. Sharp, the acknowledged best comic singer of the day; Mrs John Roe, and Mrs Aveling Smith, who also is engaged for a limited number of nights.
>
> At Nine o'Clock—THE ROTUNDA THEATRE will be thrown open, in which Tourniare's Talent Troup of Equestrians, and upwards of Forty highly-trained Horses, will make their debut, and introduce some novel and wonderful Feats of Equitation. Mr BARRY, the celebrated Clown, from Astley's, will make his first appearance in the Ring. Master of the Circle, Mr WIDDICOMB.
>
> At Ten o'Clock—The SECOND PART of the GRAND CONCERT.
>
> At Eleven o'Clock—A SPLENDID PROCESSION, presenting a faithful

representation of the Chinese Emperor and Empress reviewing their Tartar Troops before the Imperial Palace at Pekin (designed and painted by Messrs. Joseph Frederick and Alfred Adams), amidst a display of Fireworks surpassing in brilliancy all that has hitherto been attempted by that unrivalled artist, Mr Darby; in the distance, the lofty Pagodas, and monster Dragon Tower, 120 feet high, from which Joel II Diavolo will make a terrific descent, as 'Victory', on a Fiery Dragon; the whole scene terminating with a Coup de Feu of extraordinary splendour and effect, that has never yet been attempted in this or any other country.

THE ARTIFICER in the illuminating department has, during the recess prepared a number of novel devices, which will be displayed in upwards of 20,000 VARIEGATED LAMPS, throughout the Gardens.

Amongst the Pictorial Exhibitions by Mr Laidlaw, will be found Views of the Lake of Como and Taglioni's Villa; the City of Lahore at Sunset; Oberwessel, on the Rhine; and the Lake of Killarney.

THE ITALIAN WALK has been beautifully and tastefully Planted with choice shrubs, and will be brilliantly illuminated in a novel and peculiar style. [143]

In an essay on Vauxhall of 1849 Albert Smith recalled his boyhood visits and mused on the 'hybernal' existence of the gardens, what happened to them during the winter months when the sad decay eroded them further. From that bloomlessness, he wrote, Vauxhall grew a perennial flower each Whitsuntide.[144] Nine years later after the Gardens closed on 25 September 1858 the ground was sold as building property.

49   Farewell to Vauxhall
(Two handbills of 1859. Harvard University Theater Collection, VIII, 111.)

Yet Vauxhall was granted one, final fling. Its new owners gave permission for it to be reopened for a series of farewells. These were announced in *The Times* on 25 June and the first was held on Monday 18 July; there were a further seven and the Gardens closed once and for all on 25 July 1859. The following morning *The Times* carried what amounted to an obituary of 'the old-fashioned gardens'. They were, it wrote, like the 'ghost of some old friend who has been dead for some years'; Vauxhall 'is indeed hallowed by old association, but . . . so *very* old that the present generation has nothing at all to do with them [the Gardens]'.[145] On the final programmes were such old favourites as a ballet by Chapine's pupils, a concert, an equestrian performance with Henry Croueste taking part. The National Anthem was sung at the close.

50   Demolition of the Vauxhall orchestra
(J. Findlay. Watercolour, 1859. The Museum of London.)

On 22 August 1859 the auction of the property at Vauxhall Gardens began. The dancing platform realized 50 guineas, the ballet theatre (see slide 38) 17 and the orchestra, £99. Three 'deal painted tables with turned legs', made for the gardens in 1754, went for 9 shillings each. Those pictures that still remained in the supper boxes went – ironically – to the Royal Cremorne Gardens where they were installed in the Banqueting Hall.[146]

The builders were quickly at work on the twelve acre site; in 1864 St Peter, Vauxhall, was consecrated, and gradually streets of small houses covered the spot. Streets with names like Gye Street, Italian Walk and Tyers Street recall the Gardens and occupy ground within its former spaces.[147]

Since the orchestra was always the prime feature of Vauxhall Gardens, *the* familiar image around which clustered successive generations of visitors, it seemed appropriate to choose it from among Findlay's watercolours for the final slide. Findlay had been commissioned by the antiquary John Fillinham to prepare, along with H. S. Barton,[148] a full record of Vauxhall in its last moments. We have already seen the circus and stage (slide 39). Here parts of the orchestra have already been dismantled and workmen are busy upon the rest. The orchestra, of course, does not represent the theatrical history of Vauxhall as it was written during the nineteenth century, when the Gardens participated in the rounds of London entertainment. But it does symbolize the eighteenth-century contribution, which is arguably – because virtually unique in locating theatre in gardens after the old Renaissance manner of courtly entertainments – by far its most important.

BIBLIOGRAPHY

The following is a select bibliography of items most frequently cited in the notes, together with the abbreviations used there.

Altick   Richard D. Altick, *The Shows of London. A Panoramic History of Exhibitions. 1600–1862* (Cambridge, Mass., 1978).

Allen   Brian Allen, 'Jonathan Tyers's Other Garden', *Journal of Garden History*, I (1981), pp.215–38.

Bodley   Five scrapbooks and volumes of Vauxhall materials in The Bodleian Library, call mark: G. A. Surrey c.21–25.

Coke   David Coke, *The Muse's Bower. Vauxhall Gardens. 1728–1786*. Catalogue of exhibition at Gainsborough's House, Sudbury, Suffolk, 1978.

Edelstein   *Vauxhall Gardens.* A catalogue compiled by T. J. Edelstein for an exhibition at the Yale Center for British Art, New Haven, Conn., 1983.

Gowing   Lawrence Gowing, 'Hogarth, Hayman, and the Vauxhall Decorations', *Burlington Magazine*, 95 (1953), pp.4–19.

Grove   'Pleasure Gardens', *The New Grove Dictionary of Music*, ed. Stanley Sadie (London, 1980), volume XI, pp.177–81.

Guildhall   Collection of Vauxhall materials.

Harvard   Nine volumes of Vauxhall materials in the Harvard University Library Theater Collection.

Hunt   John Dixon Hunt, 'Theatres, Gardens, and Garden-theatres', *Essays and Studies 1980*, ed. Inga-Stina Ewbank (London, 1980), pp.95–118.

Rococo   *ROCOCO. Art and Design in Hogarth's England.* Catalogue of exhibition at the Victoria and Albert Museum, 1984. See especially the section on Vauxhall by David Coke, pp.74–98.

Sands   Mollie Sands, *Invitation to Ranelagh 1742–1803* (London, 1946).

Scott   W. S. Scott, *Green Retreats. The Story of Vauxhall Gardens 1661–1859* (London, 1955).

Southworth   James Granville Southworth, *Vauxhall Gardens. A Chapter in the Social History of England* (New York, 1941).

Wroth   Warwick Wroth, *The London Pleasure Gardens of the Eighteenth Century* (London, 1896; reissued, 1979).

NOTES

1   Wroth discusses over fifty pleasure gardens, in some of which 'theatrical'
     entertainments were provided; but he is not particularly concerned with the
     place of these gardens in theatre history.
2   *Journal to Stella*, ed. A. Williams (Oxford, 1948), p.272.
3   *Horace Walpole's Correspondence*, ed. W. S. Lewis and Ralph S. Brown
     (New Haven, Conn., 1941), vol.10, p.279.
4   See Ackermann, *Microcosm of London*, III (1808).
5   Wroth, pp.215–16 and 105.
6   See Altick, *passim*.
7   On this theme see *Le Lieu Théâtral à la Renaissance*, ed. Jean Jacquot, Elie
     Konigson and Marcel Oddon (Paris, 1964); *Les Fêtes de la Renaissance*, ed.
     Jean Jacquot (Paris, 1956 and 1960); and the catalogue of the exhibition, *Il
     Luogo Teatrale a Firenze* (Florence, 1975).
8   'Invented', because it is clear that the English Landscape Garden was much
     indebted to earlier, especially Italian forms and not a totally new creation as
     its early eighteenth-century proponents claimed. See also note 21 below.
9   See Mario Praz, *Conversation Pieces* (London, 1971), and Ronald Paulson,
     Emblem and Expression (London, 1975), chapter 8. On the connections
     between conversation pieces and the theatre (especially the pictorial
     representation of theatre scenes) the career of Hogarth is instructive.
10   *The Times*, 26 July, 1859. See also commentary on slide 50.
11   Wroth, pp.292–93.
12   Quoted Southworth, p.25.
13   *The Champion*, 5 August 1742.
14   Terence Hodgkinson, *Handel at Vauxhall* (London: Victoria and Albert
     Museum, n.d.).
15   [John Lockman], *A Sketch of the Spring-Gardens, Vaux-Hall in a letter to a
     noble Lord* (n.d., but probably 1751), pp.19–20.
16   For Tyers's 'other garden', see Allen.
17   Southworth and Edelstein provide more details on the layout of the
     Gardens.
18   *The Diary of John Evelyn*, ed. E. S. de Beer (Oxford, 1955), III, p.291; *The
     Diary of Samuel Pepys*, ed. R. Latham and W. Matthews (London, 1970),
     III, p.95.

19   B. de Monconys, *Voyage d'Angleterre* (1655), pt. II, pp.16–17; my translation.

20   John Aubrey, 'A Perambulation of Surrey Anno Dio 1673', Bodleian Library, MS Aubrey 4, folio 32 recto.

21   For more information on Italian Renaissance gardens and English reactions to them, see my *The Garden and the Grove. The Italian Garden in the English Imagination 1600–1750*, forthcoming 1985.

22   I have discussed this more fully elsewhere: see Hunt.

23   *The Diary*, ed. cit., II, p.393. Mondragone is illustrated in C. L. Franck, *The Villas of Frascati* (1966). For some attempt to define 'theatre' in the context of another Frascati villa, see Klaus Schwager, 'Kardinal Pietro Aldobrandinis Villa di Belvedere in Frascati', *Römisches Jahrbuch für Kunstgeschichte*, 9–10 (1961–2), pp.379–82. See also text above, p.17.

24   For the Belvedere see J. Y. S. Ackermann, 'The Belvedere as a Classical Villa', *J.W.C.I.*, XIV (1951), pp.70–91, and Hans Henrik Brummer, *The Statue Court in the Vatican Belvedere* (Stockholm, 1970); for Palestrina, the ancient Praeneste, see J. A. Hanson, *Roman Theater-Temples* (Princeton, N.J., 1959), pp.33–36.

25   'In the descent into the first garden shews itself the Colossus of Pegasus . . . or 'riseth an Island cut in the shape of a ship': Edmund Warcupp, *Italy in its Originall Glory, Ruine and Revivall* (1660), pp.309–11.

26   Lockman's *Sketch* (op. cit., note 15), quoted by Ronald Paulson, *Hogarth: His Life, Art and Times*, 2 vols. (New Haven, Connecticut, 1971), I, p.348. Paulson also recounts (I, pp.347–50) that which can be surmised about Hogarth's involvement with Tyers.

27   See Gowing, who lists the subjects of all the paintings, Edelstein, and Alastair Smart, 'Hogarth or Hayman? Another look at the *Fairies Dancing on the Green by Moonlight*', *Apollo* (March 1979), pp.208–12. All further quotations, unless otherwise identified, come from Gowing. Finally, see S. A. Henry, 'A Further Note on the Engravings of the Oil Paintings of Francis Hayman in Vauxhall Gardens', *Burlington Magazine*, 100 (1953), p.438, and *Rococo*, pp.92–96.

28   See, for example, John Ogilby, *The relation of his majestie's entertainment passing through the city of London, etc.* (1661).

29   Quoted Southworth, p.43.

30   Roy Strong, John Harris, Stephen Orgel, *The King's Arcadia* (1972), pp.197–200.

31   For more on this theme see the book announced in note 21.

32   Quoted Southworth, p.43, as for the succeeding quotation. Another trompe l'oeil painting was at the end of the vista in 1751, 'representing the Temple of *Neptune*; with his (suppos'd) Statue, standing on its Pedestal and *Tritons* underneath. Four other Deities, large as the Life, are there painted; with the same number of *Genii* or Boys, expressive of the four *Seasons*' (quoted Edelstein, p.20).

33   Southworth, p.60.

34   Quoted Hodgkinson, op. cit., note 14 above.
35   Southworth, p.43n. Wroth says the orchestra was in its final form by 1756,
      but 1758 is given by J. Timbs, *Curiosities of London*. See also Edelstein,
      pp.17–24.
36   Sybil Rosenfeld, *Georgian Scene Painters and Scene Painting* (Cambridge,
      1981), pp.32–33 (for a Vauxhall and Ranelagh represented on stage), but
      also *passim*.
37   See Roy Strong, *Splendour at Court* (1973) and A. M. Nagler, *Theatre
      Festivals of the Medici 1539 to 1637* (New Haven, Connecticut, 1964) and
      the works cited in note 7 above.
38   Mila Mastrorocco, *Le Mutazioni di Proteo. I giardini medicei del
      Cinquecento* (Florence, 1981), chapter 6.
39   See Frances Yates, *The Valois Tapestries* (1959), pp.67–69.
40   L. Châtetet-Lange, 'The Grotto of the Unicorn and the Garden of the Villa
      di Castello', *Art Bulletin*, 50 (1968), pp.51–62.
41   See Herbert Weisinger, *The Agony and the Triumph* (East Lancing,
      Michigan, 1964), pp.58–70; Richard Bernheimer, 'Theatrum Mundi', *Art
      Bulletin*, 38 (1956), pp.225–47; Jean Jacquot, 'Le Théâtre du Monde de
      Shakespeare à Calderon', *Revue de littérature comparée*, 31 (1957),
      pp.341–72.
42   Verses on slide 30. In Hunt, p.117, these were mistakenly attributed to
      Fielding.
43   See for further illustrations the second volume of Luigi Zangheri, *Pratolino:
      il giardino delle meraviglie* (Florence, 1979). Virtually nothing survives on
      the ground.
44   See for further examples Isa Belli Barsali, *La Villa a Lucca* (Rome, 1964).
45   All are illustrated and discussed in Per Bjurström, *Giacomo Torelli and
      Baroque Stage Design* (Stockholm, 1961).
46   Georgina Masson, in *Queen Christina of Sweden. Documents and Studies*,
      ed. Magnus von Platen (*Analecta Reginensia*, I, Stockholm, 1966), p.254.
47   Per Bjurström, *Feast and Theatre in Queen Christina's Rome* (Stockholm,
      1966), pp.22–23.
48   Naomi Miller, *Heavenly Caves. Reflections on the Garden Grotto* (New
      York, 1982), pp.73–76 and *passim*. For another illustration of the Versailles
      gardens *en fête* see Julia S. Berrall, *The Garden* (Penguin Books, 1978), p.186.
49   See Naomi Miller, op cit., pp.111–12 for Sanspareil.
50   Peter Holland, *The ornament of action. Text and performance in
      Restoration comedy* (Cambridge, 1979), p.36.
51   See Stephen Orgel and Roy Strong, *Inigo Jones. The Theatre of the Stuart
      Court*, 2 vols. (London, Berkeley & Los Angeles, 1973).
52   See Hunt.
53   Graham Barlow, 'Sir James Thornhill and the Theatre Royal, Drury Lane',
      The Eighteenth-Century English Stage, ed. K. Richards and P. Thomson
      (London, 1972), pp.179–93; also Sybil Rosenfeld, 'Landscape in English
      Scenery in the eighteenth century', ibid, pp.171–78.

54   Ibid, p.187.

55   Sybil Rosenfeld, *Georgian Scene Painters* . . ., pp.32–33, but also see pp.13, 24 and 35.

56   Peter Willis, *Charles Bridgeman and the English Landscape Garden* (1978) makes no mention of these theatres. That at Claremont has recently been restored by the National Trust.

57   The whole series is illustrated in John Harris, *The Artist and the Country House* (1979), pp.188–89.

58   Peter Willis, 'Jacques Rigaud's Drawings of Stowe in the Metropolitan Museum', *ECS*, 6 (1972), pp.89–98.

59   See works cited in note 9.

60   For Mercier see John Ingamells and Robert Raines, 'A Catalogue of the Paintings, Drawings and Etchings of Philip Mercier', *Walpole Society Publication*, XLVI (1976–77), pp.1–70, and the catalogue of the York City Art Gallery exhibition (1969) by the same authors.

61   For a detailed discussion of Denbies, see Allen, from whose article the following quotations are taken. Another conversation picture of Tyers and his family was sold at Sotheby's Belgravia on 31 March 1976.

62   Cited Sands, p.9.

63   Quoted from *A Trip to Vaux-Hall*; see appendix, where text is taken from Coke.

64   This is illustrated in Sands. Scott, chapter 7, surveys Vauxhall singers and their repertoire with liberal quotations. See also Grove.

65   Lockman, *A Sketch* . . ., pp.9–10, all further quotations being from this description. For the artists involved in the decoration see Edelstein and *Rococo*.

66   *A Description of Vauxhall-Gardens* (1762), p.21.

67   Ibid, p.22.

68   Southworth, p.47.

69   Ibid, p.46.

70   *Rococo*, p.84.

71   Southworth, p.140; on the food generally, ibid, pp.132–40.

72   *Comic Almanack* for 1835.

73   John Riely, *Rowlandson drawings from the Paul Mellon collection* (New Haven, Connecticut, 1978), pp.4–6 discusses another drawing of Vauxhall.

74   *Rococo*, ibid.

75   *Life of Johnson* (Oxford Standard Authors edn., 1961), p.959.

76   Scott, p.38. A possible alternative identification is not Bate Dudley but the Rev William Jackson.

77   Cited Scott, p.30. It was part of Vauxhall's carefully maintained reputation that only the 'posh' and well-to-do went there.

78   Edelstein, p.43.

79   Quoted by Aileen Ribeiro in her pioneering article, 'The exotic diversion. The dress worn at Masquerades in eighteenth-century London', *The Connoisseur* (January 1978), p.11. I am much indebted to this article for my own commentaries here.

80   *The Masquerade* (1728), cited by Ribeiro, op. cit.

81   The remark was, in fact, made of Ranelagh: see Appendix. On masquerades see Terry Castle, 'Eros and Liberty at the English Masquerades', *ECS*, 17 (1983/4), pp.156–76.

82   *Elizabeth Montagu, the Queen of the Blue Stockings*, ed. E. J. Climenson (1906), I, p.264.

83   Cited by Ribeiro, p.11.

84   As in note 80.

85   Cited by Ribeiro, p.7.

86   Ribeiro notes that several trade cards for Paulin's survive in the Heal Collection in the British Museum Print Room. Her figure 10 illustrates another, 'Jackson's Habit-Warehouse', also in Tavistock Street.

87   Sands, pp.124–25.

88   For the coiffeur see Ribeiro, p.9, and for Rogers's *Table Talk*, Scott, p.16.

89   Grove provides a useful introduction to the subject and illustrates a programme for 1786. See also R. Fiske, *English Theatre Music in the Eighteenth Century* (1973).

90   Charles Cudworth, 'The Vauxhall "Lists"', *The Galpin Society Journal*, XX (1967), pp.24–42.

91   Harvard, II, folio 92. Further details on the musical performers mentioned here may be found in Grove.

92   Walpole to Mann, 22 April 1742. In a letter to the same correspondent of 26 May he puts the cost at £16,000. *Correspondence*, ed. cit., XVII, pp.401 and 434.

93   *A Description of Ranelagh Rotunda and Gardens* (1762), p.9; further quotations unless otherwise identified, are from this text.

94   See Appendix for fuller quotations.

95   Edelstein, p.18.

96   Wroth, p.200.

97   Cited by ibid, pp. 210–11.

98   Cited by Sands, p.10. This section is much indebted to Sands.

99   Ibid, pp.211–12.

100   Wroth, pp.215–16. A painter the previous year had been one Edwards ARA.

101   Ibid, pp.94–95 and pp.93–100 for what follows.

102   See Scott, pp.113 ff. and Wroth, *passim*, for further details of these various attempts to rival the big garden-theatres.

103   Wroth illustrates the river-side entrance facing p.249.

104   Boswell, *Life of Johnson*, rev. ed. L. F. Powell (Oxford, 1950), V, pp.295–96.

105   Fillinham grangerized *Public Gardens of London*, Guildhall Library, folio 1.

106   Ibid, folio 5.

107   Sidney Garden, Vauxhall watercolour plan, Guildhall Library, P small boards.

108   *Walpole Correspondence*, ed. cit., 10, p.314.

109   See Grove, also for Russian example cited later.

110   *Travels of Carl Philipp Moritz in England in 1782* (1924), pp.39–40.

111   See F. Gruber, 'Les "Vauxhalls" parisiens au XVIIIe siècle', *Bulletin de la Société de l'Histoire de l'Art francais*, forthcoming.

112   *Eighteenth-century French drawings from the Musée Carnavalet*, catalogue for the exhibition at the National Academy of Design (New York, 1979), p.20. See also Edelstein, p.48.

113   Quoted Southworth, p.71.

114   British Library playbills 377.

115   Quoted Southworth, p.86.

116   Quoted ibid, p.89, as for the other details given here.

117   See Southworth,pp.61 ff.

118   Cited Scott, p.83.

119   John Forster, *Life of Dickens* (1966), II, p.81.

120   A. H. Coxe, 'The lesser-known circuses of London', *Theatre Notebook*, 13 (1959), pp.89–100, where an engraving of the Vauxhall circus ring is illustrated; George Speaight, 'The circus at Vauxhall Gardens', *Theatre Notebook*, 29 (1975), p.1.

121   Southworth, p.4.

122   Cutting of 1823 in Bodley: G. A. Surrey C.23 following f.33.

123   See Alan St. H. Brock, *A History of Fireworks* (1949).

124   Harvard, IV, f.122.

125   Ibid, III, f.44.

126   Altick, p.345.

127   Harvard, III, ff.50 and 88. For the stage work of Clarkson Stanfield see the 1979 catalogue of the exhibition mounted by Tyne and Wear Metropolitan District Museums, especially pp.23-29 and *passim*.

128   Harvard, IV, f.19.

129   Altick, p.330.

130   Harvard, VII, f.122 and IV, f.8 respectively.

131   Altick, pp.47 and 278–79; see also Harvard, VI, f.28. For a Dickensian connection see Malcolm Morley, 'Jim Crow and Boz's Juba', *The Dickensian*, XLVII (1950–51), pp.28 ff.

132   Scott, p.95; Wroth gives the date as 1835.

133   Quoted Scott, pp.63 ff.

134   H. H. Montgomery, *The History of Kensington* (1889), p.104.

135   Altick, pp.472 ff.

136   Harvard, V, f.75.

137   Eighteen issues are held in the Bromhead Collection at the University of London Senate House Library; Wroth (p.322) says there were only sixteen.

138   See the catalogue of the Loutherbourg Exhibition (Greater London Council, 1973) and R. G. Allen, *The Stage Spectacles of . . . Loutherbourg*, unpub. thesis, Yale University, 1960.

139   Altick, p.320.

140   Quoted ibid, pp.322–23.

141   Ibid, p.330.
142   Southworth, p.174 and Harvard, VII, f.50.
143   Quoted Scott, pp.102–04.
144   *Sketches of London Life and Character* (1859), pp.149–58.
145   Quoted Southworth, pp.179–81.
146   Wroth, p.324; also Southworth, p.181.
147   Wroth, pp.324–25; also Southworth, pp.181–82.
148   *Rococo*, p.97.

APPENDIX

Selections of literary descriptions of the Gardens at Vauxhall followed by two accounts of Ranelagh. Please note that original spellings have been retained.

1   Joseph Addison, 'The Spectator', no. 383 (20 May 1712)

As I was sitting in my chamber, and thinking on a subject for my next *Spectator*, I heard two or three irregular bounces at my Landlady's door, and upon the opening of it, a loud cheerful voice enquiring whether the Philosopher was at home. The child who went to the door answered very innocently, that he did not lodge there. I immediately recollected that it was my good friend Sir ROGER's voice; and that I had promised to go with him on the water to *Spring-garden*, in case it proved a good evening. The Knight put me in mind of my promise from the stair-case, but told me that if I was speculating, he would stay below till I had done. Upon my coming down, I found all the children of the family got about my old friend, and my Landlady herself, who is a notable prating gossip, engaged in a conference with him; being mightily pleased with his stroaking her little boy upon the head, and bidding him be a good child, and mind his book.

      We were no sooner come to the *Temple* stairs, but we were surrounded with a crowd of water-men, offering their respective services. Sir ROGER, after having looked about him very attentively, spied one with a wooden-leg, and immediately gave him orders to get his boat ready. As we were walking towards it, *You must know*, says Sir ROGER, *I never make use of any body to row me, that has not either lost a leg or an arm. I would rather bate him a few strokes of his Oar, than not employ a honest man that has been wounded in the Queen's service. If I was a Lord or a Bishop, and kept a Barge, I would not put a fellow in my livery that had not a wooden-leg.*

      My old friend, after having seated himself, and trimmed the boat with his coachman, who, being a very sober man, always serves for Ballast on these occasions, we made the best of our way for *Fox-hall*. Sir ROGER obliged the Waterman to give us the history of his right leg, and hearing that he had left it at *La Hogue*, with many particulars which passed in that glorious action, the Knight in the triumph of his heart made several reflections on the greatness of the *British* nation; as, that one *Englishman* could beat three *Frenchmen*; that we could never be in danger of popery so long as we took care of our fleet; that the *Thames* was the noblest river in *Europe*; that *London-bridge* was a greater piece of work than any of the seven wonders of the world; with many other honest prejudices which naturally cleave to the heart of a true *Englishman*.

After some short pause, the old Knight turning his head twice or thrice, to take a survey of this great Metropolis, bid me observe how thick the city was set with churches, and that there was scarce a single steeple on this side *Temple-bar. A most heathenish sight!* says Sir ROGER: *There is no religion at this end of the town. The fifty new churches will very much mend the prospect; but church-work is slow, church-work is slow!*

I do not remember I have any where mentioned in Sir ROGER's character, his custom of saluting every body that passes him with a good-morrow or a good-night. This the old man does out of the overflowings of humanity, though at the same time it renders him so popular among all his country neighbours, that it is thought to have gone a good way in making him once or twice Knight of the shire. He cannot forbear this exercise of benevolence even in town, when he meets with any one in his morning or evening walk. It broke from him to several boats that passed by us upon the water; but to the Knight's great surprize, as he gave the good-night to two or three young fellows a little before our landing, one of them, instead of returning the civility, asked us what queer old Putt we had in the boat, and whether he was not ashamed to go a wenching at his years? with a great deal of the like *Thames*-ribaldry. Sir ROGER seemed a little shocked at first, but at length assuming a face of magistracy, told us, *That if he were a* Middlesex *Justice, he would make such vagrants know that her Majesty's subjects were no more to be abused by water than by land.*

We were now arrived at *Spring-garden*, which is exquisitely pleasant at this time of year. When I considered the fragrancy of the walks and bowers, with the choirs of birds that sung upon the trees, and the loose tribe of people that walked under their shades, I could not but look upon the place as a kind of *Mahometan* paradise. Sir ROGER told me it put him in mind of a little coppice by his house in the country, which his Chaplain used to call an Aviary of Nightingales. *You must understand*, says the Knight, *there is nothing in the world that pleases a man in love so much as your Nightingale. Ah, Mr.* SPECTATOR! *the many moonlight nights that I have walked by my self, and thought on the widow by the musick of the Nightingale!* He here fetched a deep sigh, and was falling into a fit of musing, when a mask, who came behind him, gave him a gentle tap upon the shoulder, and asked him if he would drink a bottle of Mead with her? But the Knight being startled at so unexpected a familiarity, and displeased to be interrupted in his thoughts of the widow, told her, *She was a wanton baggage*, and bid her go about her business.

We concluded our walk with a glass of *Burton*-ale, and a slice of Hung-beef. When we had done eating our selves, the Knight called a Waiter to him, and bid him carry the remainder to a Waterman that had but one leg. I perceived the fellow stared upon him at the oddness of the message, and was going to be saucy; upon which I ratified the Knight's commands with a peremptory look.

As we were going out of the garden, my old friend thinking himself obliged, as a member of the *Quorum*, to animadvert upon the morals of the place, told the Mistress of the house, who sat at the bar, That he should be a better customer to her garden, if there were more Nightingales and fewer Strumpets.

2   A Trip to Vaux-Hall: or, a General Satyr on the Thames (London, 1737)

To please two Punks, who freely share their Bounties;
Mercantile one, and one a rampant Countess,
Who taste, without reserve, each tempting Joy
And whom Live's luscious Banquet ne'er can cloy;
Our Vehicle prepar'd at Whitehall Stairs,
And both the Whores deckt out in all their Airs;
Lolling in State with one on either Side,
And gently falling, with the Wind and Tide;
Last Night, the Evening of a sultry Day,
I sail'd, triumphant, on the liquid Way,
To hear the Fidlers of Spring-Gardens play;
To see the Walks, Orchestra, Colonades;
The Lamps and Trees in mingled Lights and Shades.
The Scene so new, with Pleasure and Surprise,
Feasted awhile our ravished Ears and Eyes.
The motley Croud we next with Care survey,
The Young, the Old, the Splenetic and Gay:
The Fop emasculate, the rugged Brave,
All jumbled here, as in the common Grave.
Here sat a Group of 'Prentices, and there
The awkward daughters of a late Lord Mayor;
Next them a Country Bumpkin and his Cousin,
And, stuck about, Red-Ribbon'd Knights a Dozen;
Like ruddy Pinks, or Gilly-flowers in Pots;
'Mongst Bawds, and Rakes, and Semptresses and Sots.
         Here sits my Lord with Vest of Gold emboss'd;
And there his Taylor sighing for the Cost.
One Month will see him to that Prison sent
Where, six Months pass'd, his Lordship's Butcher went.
His Children starving on the Parish Care,
My Lord has left them now no better Fare.
No Matter – tho' he's in the Butcher's Books,
His Bills unpaid, not so his new French Cooks;
Besides my Lord, when he was to be paid,
Had lost six Hundred Pounds at the Masquerade.
Had given Faranelli fifty more,
And laid out twenty in a Monkey for his Whore.
What are to him the Pangs of Vulgar Souls!
No Thought of those a Noble's Joys controuls.
Let petty Cheats, who drive in humble Hack,
Dreâd Duns, they've no Protection to their Back.
But to return, and ramble round the Gardens,

His Lordship's Morals leave, not worth five Farthings.
      And meet two Parsons, kept at constant Hire,
Domestick Chaplains of my Landlord
Who, waddling with a Load of Guts before 'em,
Are, by their holy Looks to keep Decorum.
For whatsoe're the Doctors do in private,
No open Vice, but one, they will connive at.
      The doating Cit here hugs his wanton Wife,
Calls her his Sweeting Fubsey, Duck and Life,
Nor grudges Ham, tho' fourteen Pence an Ounce,
Whilst Horns she's making o'er the Cuckold's Sconce:
But to the Captain gives such am'rous Leers,
As shew her Heart in his, and not her Dear's.
Tho' to this Grocer but two Winters wed,
Three 'Prentices at Home have shar'd his Bed;
Abroad Six honest Countrymen of mine,
And of the Army Blades some thirty-nine.
      See yonder gay Flirtilla laughing walk,
And with embroider'd Strephon seems to talk;
Each Syllable she utters, hollows loud,
She answers him, but speaks to all the Croud.
This Couple for each other are design'd,
But she is making Love to all Mankind.
And he, whose only View in Wedlock's Pelf,
Can find no Charms in any but Himself.
The dear, dear Looking-Glass, his sole Delight,
No others Eyes so black, no Teeth so white.
      Next there is haughty Zara, moving slow,
The Company, she says, are mean and low:
Wonders, Good Heavens! how she chanc'd to come,
'Mong such a Mob, so very far from Home:
This may seem decent Pride — but not to all,
'Cause some have known her Father's Cobling Stall.
      Observe with what a fond paternal Care,
Yon courteous Knight beholds his Son and Heir,
Pleas'd with his stupid Look, in Rapture cries,
In Time this Boy'll teach Wisdom to the Wise!
His Brilliant Parts in Time shall Nations glad,
In short, he'll be the Picture of his Dad,
My Lady laughing in her Sleeve this while;
Casts on the real Dad an am'rous Smile;
But's somewhat shock'd her Hero to explore,
Pent up in Coop with forty Footmen more:
Oh that I were, cries she, with honest Saul,
Taller than other Men, or with 'em all!

But barr'd from thence she turns her View,
On the smug Waiter, with his Apron blue;
The painted Tin upon his rising Crest,
Pleases her Sight, and warms her am'rous Breast.
Not the blue Ribbon, with fam'd Edward's Star,
Can with this Tapster's Clout and Badge compare,
At Home, perhaps, with more than common Joy,
She'll hug her Knight, whilst dreaming of this Toy.
He to reward her Love, and keep it still,
Next Morn presents some Jewel or some Bill,
This sold or chang'd, Eftsoons a Part is sent
To Tom, who guess'd last Night, at what she meant.
An Assignation's made by trusty Nancy
Unless some other Slave first strikes her Fancy.
   The Knight, his Lady and their hopeful Son,
Thus reconnoitred, let us now pass on,
And fix'd our Eyes upon a Man of Worship,
Who runs a-muck, and worries Men, as Curs Sheep.
Who gets by daily Warrants daily Bread,
The Benches Honour, and his Neighbour's Dread.
Emblem of Justice! ruling in the Dark,
Who neither reads nor writes but sets his Mark,
And leaves all learned Drudg'ry to his Clerk.
This Man who traded once in Soap and Candles,
Now all the Business of his Parish handles,
Handles indeed! but roughly you may say,
And, to increase his Wealth, makes Beggars pay.
No Stocks nor Whipping Post but can declare
His Mercy to all Wretches in Despair.
What Grizzly Forms are these, who Centry stand,
With glouting Looks, and Mopstick in one hand?
Priests of Diana set to guard the Grove
'Gainst Venus and her Son, the God of Love:
For such the furious Heat of English Dames,
And such the Swains ungovernable Flames,
That yet they any how but under Shelter,
Shameless! they'll all go to it helter skelter.
   See modest Fulvia, how demure she sits!
One Word indecent throws her into Fits;
The Touch of Man will discompose her quite,
Yet in the Water she indur'd the Sight,
Nor could the Fan display'd conceal her strong Delight
With Head oft turning to the fading Shore,
She looks, and looks, till she can see no more;
Unless some other Triton of the Flood

Starts up to charm her with a Scene as good.
Again her Eye-Balls roll, her Soul's on Fire,
Nor Thames himself can quench her hot Desire.
With Fulvia's Modesty exactly suits
The Virtue of her Brothers, those two Brutes,
Who, both in places, each a large Estate
Behold their Father thro' a Prison-Grate.
   Of swarthy Jews, next these, a greasy Croud,
Against Extortion are declaiming loud;
'Tis hard to give a Shilling none knows why,
The wet was right, but damn the Shilling dry.
The Thing's too serious to be nam'd in Scoff,
'Twas just put on when't should be taken off.
Musick may be, perhaps, of Love the Food,
But right old Port or Florence Wine's as good.
They wonder'd what the Christian Jew could mean!
But had these stiff-neck'd Israelites e'er seen,
And seen, could any how contrive to read
The cogent Reasons why this Law's decreed;
They'd own them full of Truth, and Wit, and Sense;
and far out-doing Tully's Eloquence:
The Vaux-hall style so pure, no Sentence harsh,
That Rome and Athens now must yield to Lambeth-Marsh.
Rot his Reas'ning (cries Friend Abr'ham,) all Stuff!
Forge Tickets in ten minutes! Time enough.
Then to proclaim his Waiters Rogues aloud!
Why not? You'll find more Rogues among the Croud.
Your Pocket may be pick'd by some Lac'd Lord;
If so, the Caution's good, and safe's the Word.
   But why this Rout about a lousy Shilling?
Keep out, and sh----t, cries T-- if you're not willing.
In England now can Musick be too dear,
The Fiddles of all Italy transplanted here?
They strive to charm not Souls that grudge their Chink:
And Musick ne'er was fram'd for Men who think:
Or would so many thoughtless Boobies run
To squeaking Op'ra's til they're half undone?
Or Ladies worship Farri as a God?
Who, say some Criticks, rather is a Rod,
Or Scourge to lash the Follies of the Age,
And drive all Sense and Virtue from the Stage.

3   From 'Scots Magazine', July and August, 1739

We find so much difficulty, at present, to render this season of the year tolerable, in point of pleasure and entertainment, that there is some difficulty in accounting for that chearfulness which we meet with in the writings of our forefathers on the *approach of spring*, and the *evening breezes* of *June* and *July*: for, so far are the *beau monde* from prizing the charms which nature has so long disclosed, without *any variation*, that the simple *woods* and *groves*, the *meads* and *purling streams*, have lost the power to please: And the additions made to these, to render them more capable of yielding delight, are such, as for many centuries were judged *ridiculous* in themselves, and *irreconcileable* with our genius and clime: but thanks to the assistance of some kind visitors from *other nations*, we have surmounted the difficulties nature and custom laid in our way, and *Italian ridotto's* have been seen amongst us, spite of the inclemency of *evening damps* or *British rusticity*.

The annual improvements in *Vaux-Hall* gardens, and the great resort of personages of the first rank, have, for the five last years, drawn a multitude of people together every fine evening during the entertainment of those honoured walks; and the practice of having tickets for the season, to admit two persons every night, does not a little add to the number of the company, by putting it in a Gentleman's power, for so small a charge, to oblige his friends with so generally approved an amusement. The price of admittance, without a ticket, is one shilling for each person; from which last article alone it is computed, that one night with another, not less than *one thousand* shillings are received each evening of performance during the season.

Your distance from a kind of entertainment so new amongst us, and so much approved, especially by the Ladies, may make an account of it acceptable to such of your readers as have a taste for polite amusements:— Wherefore, in order to give a more perfect idea of the time spent in this fashionable diversion, the most natural method I can think of, will be to divide the three hours, usually bestowed on a visit to this melodious grove, into separate articles, and under each to give the truest description I can of the manner in which it is employed.—It will not be amiss to apprise you of its lying on the other side of the river from *London* and *Westminster*, about a mile from the first mentioned city.—The three hours are those from *seven* to *ten*.
Note – the description of only two of the three hours is reproduced here.

The First Hour
About *Westminster* and *Whitehall* stairs, barges with six or four oars each, attend (hired, most of them, at ten shillings for the barge, and a crown each oar for the evening) till the Ladies have done tea: by the help of coaches, chairs, &c. about *seven* they arrive at the water-side; and with many expressions, and some apprehension of danger, they are, by the aid of the Gentlemen who accompany them, and the watermens assistance, got on board; and *Tom*, who generally can blow the *French* horn, is placed exactly with his back against his Lady's shoulders. The putting off the barge from shore occasions several *Oh's!* and gives opportunity for any kind fair-one to distinguish her favourite by a close cling to his side, and a pinch in the arm.—After repeated cautions to the watermen to take care, the vessel leaves the shore; and the air proves sharp enough to oblige the

Ladies to vail their necks by the envious cloud of a handkerchief, tied with such a designed carelesness, as gives even a grace to that impertinent screen of beauty.—*Tom* plays an air from the last new Opera; and the company regale themselves with a glass of citron or plague-water, or ratafie; and Miss *Kitty*, by mamma's command, sings the last song her master, *Sig. C——i* taught her, with the applause of all present; her papa being engaged elsewhere for the evening.—Several boats with young Gentlemen only, approach within oar-length, and ogle the Ladies; who, with a pleas'd disdain, correct their freedom; and both agreeably part, in hope of second interview in the gardens.

At *Somerset* (the place to take water from *Covent-Garden*) and the *Temple* stairs, a number of young fellows are hurrying into boats; who, though they set out by themselves, seldom return without female companions.

At all the stairs from the *Temple* down to the *Bridge* the watermen are busily employed in taking their company on board; which consists of various degrees. Sir *John*, from *Fenchurch-street*, with his Lady and whole family of children, is attended by a footman, with a hand-basket well cramm'd with provisions for the voyage. The boat sallies a little at setting off; but the Knight laughs at the fear of his spouse and the young Ladies his daughters, declaring, the danger that scares them to be nothing, compared to what he came through in his last voyage from *Oporto*. Misses give an entertaining account of dress and choice of partners at the last city-ball; which, tho' mamma smiles at, Sir *John* corrects, with doubting whether they gave equal attention to the sermons they hear; which his youngest daughter answers prettily enough, by assuring him, for her sisters and self, that they do not take more notice of people in any place whatever than at church.—My Lady grows sick; a glass of wine and drops (no water being in the boat) is instantly given her; and on her recovery, eldest Miss cuts the cake, and distributes it among the company, and a glass of wine is drank round.

At the next stairs, Mr. *William*, an apprentice in *Cheapside*, by the contrivance of her confident, who accompanies them, is taking water with Miss *Suckey*, his master's daughter, who is supposed to be gone next door to drink tea, and he to meet an uncle coming out of the country. The thought of having deceived the old people makes them laugh immoderately along the street, and almost totter over the boat instead of getting into it. They are no sooner seated, and got from shore, with hearty wishes that they may meet no body that knows them, than the Ladies find, one of them through hurry had forgotten her handkerchief, and the other her snuff-box. The subject that employs them the whole passage is the admirable thought and contrivance that brought them out with such secrecy.—The watermen beg leave to stop to drink, which is denied, on account of their not having seen the gardens this year, and being obliged, at all events, to reach home by *ten*.

An honest old mechanick and his spouse come next. He assures her his Royal Highness himself favours *Vaux Hall* with his presence almost every week; and that it is said to be so much improved since he was a young man, that he was resolved to see what new-fangled notions they had got now-a-days, to exceed what were in fashion then. He gives the watermen some drink, asks their names, whether they are married or single, how many children they have alive, &c. which, with the frequent interruption of observations on the companies that overtake them, and descriptions of the barges they pass, fills up the time of their voyage.

Being all landed, they proceed in cavalcade, through a lane of watermen, to the entrance of the gardens; where, (no dogs being admitted) after *Chlo* is huff'd by one passage-keeper, *Pug* beat by another, and *Pompey* scar'd by a third, they are all trusted to the care of their several watermen; and after shewing tickets, or paying money, the Ladies and Gentlemen walk in, survey the coop made to keep the footmen in, just at the door, take a hasty circuit round the walks, the paintings not being yet let down, take a view of *Handel*'s bust, curiously carved on a fine block of marble, and plac'd on one side of the garden, striking his lyre:– but before they have observed half its beauties, the musick striking up, the whole company crowd from every part of the gardens toward the orchestra and organ; which gives a fair opportunity of meeting one's acquaintance, and remarking what beaus, bells, and beauties are present; a part of the diversion as agreeable as any to,

Sir, your humble servant,

S. TOUPEE

The Second Hour

After the piece of musick is finish'd, a silence ensues, of a length sufficient to allow the company time to take a circuit of the gardens before another begins; which is the same before each piece; and those intervals are chiefly employed in visiting the walks, remarking the company, and viewing the paintings, which have been put up the last spring to protect the Ladies, while sitting in the arbours, from catching cold in their necks by the inclemency of the evening breezes.—These paintings forming something like three parts of a square, the Prince's pavilion (so called in honour of his Royal Highness, who always honours that place with his presence when he visits these gardens) and the house belonging to the manager, form the fourth. In the middle of this square, which takes up about a fourth part of the gardens, stands a beautiful orchestra for the band of musick, which consists of the best hands upon every instrument in modern use: and from that a little bridge of four or five yards reaches to an elegant edifice, wherein is placed an excellent organ; which has lately been fitted to several new pieces of entertainment, particularly a *symphony of singing-birds*, which never fails to meet with the loud applause of all present. Many little novelties are contrived to yield a greater variety to the audience on the other instruments; and a *set of small bells* have been introduced in a tune which meets with a very favourable reception.—The walks leading close by the front of the arbours, (each of which is large enough to entertain ten or twelve persons to supper) the paintings at the back of every arbour afford a very entertaining view; especially when the Ladies, as ought ever to be contrived, sit with their heads against them. And, what adds not a little to the pleasure of these pictures, they give an unexceptionable opportunity of gazing on any pleasing fair-one, without any other pretence than the credit of a fine taste for the piece behind her.—To preserve these pieces from the weather, they are fixed so as to be in cases, contrived on purpose, from the close of the entertainment every night, to the fifth tune of the evening following; after which, in an instant, they all fall down; and from an open rural view, the eye is relieved by the agreeable surprize of some of the most favourite fancies of our poets in the most remarkable scenes of our comedies, some of the celebrated dancers, &c. in their most remarkable attitudes, several of the childish diversions, and other whims that are well enough liked by most people at a time they are *disposed to smile*, and everything of a light kind, and tending to *unbend the thoughts*, has an effect *desired* before it is *felt*.

By the time the next piece is begun, the gardens being pretty full, the company crowd round the musick; and, by being forced to stand close, have an opportunity of taking a strict observation of every face near, and, as it frequently happens, of picking out companions for the remaining part of the ———— evening.—Sir *John Trot* points out to his Lady, who has not before crossed the water for twenty years, the motion of the Gentleman who beats time, the manly strokes of the Kettle-drummer, and the wonderful strength of lungs with which Mr *S*—— sounds the trumpet. The *Petit Maitres*, at the beginning of a solo on the last mention'd instrument, fixing their toes in a proper position, pull out their snuff-boxes; and, after an emphatical nod at setting off, take a pinch in exact time; till the martial notes raising, by *slow degrees*, their untried courage, they discharge the whole force of their valour upon the eyes of the Ladies who stand next them; who, generally, receive their fire with great resolution, and make a defence often fatal to the assailants. Mrs *Flimsy* finds in the *softer musick* something so like the ravishing softness of the *Italian opera's*, that, in an extasy of pleasure at the bewitching notes, she is upon the point of falling, when the young Lord *Shallow*, with a complaisance hereditary in his family, interposing his kind hand, startles her with an agreeable surprize, and occasions as many *apologies for the freedom* on one hand, and *acknowledgements for the obligation* on the other, as, by a mutual display of the most engaging rhetorick, lay the foundation of an acquaintance that lasts, perhaps, for some hours.—Gentlemen who come alone are open to the overtures of any amiable companion, and Ladies who venture without a masculine guide, are not, generally speaking, averse to the company of a polite protector.—The music again ceasing, and dusk approaching, the green walks are filled; at the termination of which stands a man in the posture of a Constable, to protect the Ladies from any insult, &c. and at the bottom of the grand walks, and by the help of a ha-ha wall, the top of which, standing in a trench, is on a level with the ground, the prospect is open to the country, and a hideous figure of *Aurora* on a pedestal *interrupts*, I cannot say *terminates* the view. Soft whispers begin now to murmur thro' the trees; and, the shade of evening favouring the Ladies with a convenience of blushing without being perceived, or of avoiding any hard thought for omitting that pleasing mark of innocence on occasions when it may happen to be expected, the lofty trees, which form a grove that must be called *delightful*, and every fanning breeze, by waving the garments of the sylvan Deities (the only ones we know) yield a double delight, and resemble, as much as we can guess at this distance of time, the most delightful scenes of old *Arcadia*: And when the musick plays at a distance, so as to be heard thro' the leaves in *one connected sound*, without any distinction of one instrument from another, the inchanting harmony produces a pleasure scarce to be equalled by nature, not easy to be conceived in imagination;—and I cannot help confessing that, according to what I can judge from my own experience, the breast must be a stranger to passion that feels not a *tender biass* to love, and a *powerful one indeed* if any *object of affection* chance to be near; for every return of the artful symphony thro' any chance vacancy of the grove, fresh fans the glowing fame, and irresistibly increases the influence of the fair-one, who yet has more charms added by every melting effect the melody has on her mind and gesture. In this situation, if *soft* *ideas* prevail more than elsewhere, those only will wonder at it whose minds are proof against *Cupid's* painful delight, and whose ears are deaf to the power of harmony, and arm'd against all the accidental motives to love that are apt to prevail upon a mind *bent on pleasure.*—A few turns round the shades makes the Ladies glad to think of sitting down to rest themselves; and the Gentlemen assiduously seek the most agreeable arbours to regale them with a repast suitable in elegance to the elevation of their ideas; which usually happening about nine o'clock, the description thereof will naturally fall into the next letter you receive from,

SIR, *Your humble servant,*

S. TOUPEE

4 Oliver Goldsmith, 'The Citizen of the World' (1762), letter LXXI

From Lien Chi Altangi, to Fum Hoam, first president of the Ceremonial Academy at Pekin, in China.

The People of *London* are as fond of walking as our friends at *Pekin* of riding; one of the principal entertainments of the citizens here in summer is to repair about nightfall to a garden not far from town, where they walk about, shew their best cloaths and best faces, and listen to a concert provided for the occasion.

I accepted an invitation a few evenings ago from my old friend, the man in black, to be one of a party that was to sup there, and at the appointed hour waited upon him at his lodgings. There I found the company assembled and expecting my arrival. Our party consisted of my friend in superlative finery, his stockings rolled, a black velvet waistcoat which was formerly new, and his grey wig combed down in imitation of hair. A pawn-broker's widow, of whom, by the bye, my friend was a professed admirer, dressed out in green damask with three gold rings on every finger. Mr. *Tibbs* the second rate beau, I have formerly described, together with his lady, in flimsy silk, dirty gauze instead of linen, and an hat as big as an umbrello.

Our first difficulty was in settling how we should set out. Mrs. *Tibbs* had a natural aversion to the water, and the widow being a little in flesh, as warmly protested against walking, a coach was therefore agreed upon; which being too small to carry five, Mr. *Tibbs* consented to sit in his wife's lap.

In this manner therefore we set forward, being entertained by the way with the bodings of Mr. *Tibbs*, who assured us, he did not expect to see a single creature for the evening above the degree of a cheesemonger; that this was the last night of the gardens, and that consequently we should be pestered with the nobility and gentry from *Thames-street* and *Crooked-lane*, with several other prophetic ejaculations, probably inspired by the uneasiness of his situation.

The illuminations began before we arrived, and I must confess, that upon entering the gardens, I found every sense overpaid with more than expected pleasure; the lights every where glimmering through the scarcely moving trees; the full-bodied consort bursting on the stillness of the night; the natural consort of the birds, in the more retired part of the grove, vying with that which was formed by art; the company gayly dressed looking satisfaction; and the tables spread with various delicacies, all conspired to fill my imagination with the visionary happiness of the *Arabian* lawgiver, and lifted me into an ecstasy of admiration. Head of *Confucius*, cried I to my friend, this is fine! this unites rural beauty with courtly magnificence, if we except the virgins of immortality that hang on every tree, and may be plucked at every desire, I don't see how this falls short of *Mahomet's Paradise!* As for virgins, cries my friend, it is true, they are a fruit that don't much abound in our gardens here; but if ladies as plenty as apples in autumn, and as complying as any *houry* of them all can content you, I fancy we have no need to go to heaven for Paradise.

I was going to second his remarks when we were called to a consultation by Mr. Tibbs and the rest of the company, to know in what manner we were to lay out the evening to the greatest advantage. Mrs. Tibbs was for keeping the genteel walk of the garden, where she observed there was always the very best company; the widow, on the contrary, (who came but once a season) was for securing a good standing place to see the water-works, which she assured us would begin in less than an hour at farthest; a dispute therefore began, and as it was managed between two of very opposite characters, it threatened to grow more bitter at every reply. Mrs. Tibbs wondered how people could pretend to know the polite world who had received all their rudiments of breeding behind a compter; to which the other replied, that tho' some people sat behind compters, yet they could sit at the head of their own tables too, and carve three good dishes of hot meat whenever they thought proper, which was more than some people could say for themselves, that hardly knew a rabbet and onions from a green goose and gooseberries. It is hard to say where this might have ended, had not the husband, who probably knew the impetuosity of his wife's disposition, proposed to end the dispute by adjourning to a box, and try if there was any thing to be had for supper that was supportable. To this we all consented, but there a new distress arose, Mr. and Mrs. Tibbs would sit in none but a genteel box, a box where they might see and be seen, one, as they expressed it, in the very focus of public view; but such a box was not easy to be obtained, for tho' we were perfectly convinced of our own gentility, and the gentility of our appearance, yet we found it a difficult matter to persuade the keepers of the boxes to be of our opinion; they chose to reserve genteel boxes for what they judged more genteel company.

At last however we were fixed, tho' somewhat obscurely, and supplied with the usual entertainment of the place. The widow found the supper excellent, but Mrs. Tibbs thought every thing detestable: come, come, my dear, cries the husband, by way of consolation, to be sure we can't find such dressing here as we have at lord Crumps or lady Crimps; but for Vauxhall dressing it is pretty good, it is not their victuals indeed I find fault with, but their wine; their wine, cries he, drinking off a glass, indeed, is most abominable.

By this last contradiction the widow was fairly conquered in point of politeness. She perceived now that she had no pretensions in the world to taste, her very senses were vulgar, since she had praised detestable custard, and smacked at wretched wine; she was therefore content to yield the victory, and for the rest of the night to listen and improve. It is true she would now and then forget herself and confess she was pleased, but they soon brought her back again to miserable refinement. She once praised the painting of the box in which we were sitting, but was soon convinced that such paltry pieces ought rather to excite horror than satisfaction; she ventured again to commend one of the singers, but Mrs. Tibbs soon let her know, in the style of a connoisseur, that the singer in question had neither ear, voice, nor judgment.

Mr. Tibbs now willing to prove that his wife's pretensions to music were just, entreated her to favour the company with a song; but to this she gave a positive denial, for you know very well, my dear, says she, that I am not in voice to day, and when ones voice is not equal to ones judgment, what signifies singing; besides as there is no accompanyment, it would be but spoiling music. All these excuses however were overruled by the rest of the company who, though one would think they already had music enough, joined in the entreaty. But particularly the widow, now willing to convince the company of her breeding, pressed so warmly that she seem'd determined to take no refusal. At last then the lady complied, and after humming for some minutes, began with such a voice and such affectation, as I could perceive gave but little satisfaction to any except her husband. He sate with rapture in his eye, and beat time with his hand on the table. Mrs. Tibbs therefore kept on singing, and we continued to listen, till at last, when the song was just concluded, the waiter came to inform us that the water-works were over.

The water-works over, cried the widow! the water-works over already, that's impossible, they can't be over so soon! It is not my business, replied the fellow, to contradict your ladyship, I'll run again and see; he went, and soon returned with a confirmation of the dismal tidings. No ceremony could now bind my friend's disappointed mistress, she testifed her displeasure in the openest manner; in short, she now began to find fault in turn, and at last insisted upon going home, just at the time that Mr. and Mrs. Tibbs assured the company, that the polite hours were going to begin, and that the ladies would instantaneously be entertained with the horns.   Adieu.

5   Tobias Smollett, 'Humphry Clinker' (1771), two letters on Vauxhall from Matthew Branble and Lydia Melford

The diversions of the times are not ill suited to the genius of this incongruous monster, called *the public*. Give it noise, confusion, glare, and glitter; it has no idea of elegance and propriety – What are the amusements of Ranelagh? One half of the company are following at the other's tails, in an eternal circle; like so many blind asses in an olive-mill, where they can neither discourse, distinguish, nor be distinguished; while the other half are drinking hot water, under the denomination of tea, till nine or ten o'clock at night, to keep them awake for the rest of the evening. As for the orchestra, the vocal music especially, it is well for the performers that they cannot be heard distinctly. Vauxhall is a composition of baubles, overcharged with paltry ornaments, ill conceived, and poorly executed; without any unity of design, or propriety of disposition. It is an unnatural assembly of objects, fantastically illuminated in broken masses; seemingly contrived to dazzle the eyes and divert the imagination of the vulgar – Here a wooden lion, there a stone statue; in one place, a range of things like coffeehouse boxes, covered a-top; in another, a parcel of ale-house benches; in a third, a puppet-show representation of a tin cascade; in a fourth, a gloomy cave of a circular form, like a sepulchral vault half lighted; in a fifth, a scanty flip of grass-plat, that would not afford pasture sufficient for an ass's colt. The walks, which nature seems to have intended for solitude, shade, and silence, are filled with crowds of noisy people, sucking up the nocturnal rheums of an aguish climate; and through these gay scenes, a few lamps glimmer like so many farthing candles.

When I see a number of well dressed people, of both sexes, sitting on the covered benches, exposed to the eyes of the mob; and, which is worse, the cold, raw, night-air, devouring sliced beef, and swilling port, and punch, and cyder, I can't help compassionating their temerity; while I despise their want of taste and decorum; but, when they course along those damp and gloomy walks, or crowd together upon the wet gravel, without any other cover than the cope of Heaven, listening to a song, which one half of them cannot possibly hear, how can I help supposing they are actually possessed by a spirit, more absurd and pernicious than any thing we meet with in the precincts of Bedlam? In all probability, the proprietors of this, and other public gardens of inferior note, in the skirts of the metropolis, are, in some shape, connected with the faculty of physic, and the company of undertakers; for, considering that eagerness in the pursuit of what is called pleasure, which now predominates through every rank and denomination of life, I am persuaded that more gouts, rheumatisms, catarrhs, and consumptions are caught in these nocturnal pastimes, *sub dio*, than from all the risques and accidents to which a life of toil and danger is exposed.

But even these superb objects are not so striking as the crowds of people that swarm in the streets. I at first imagined that some great assembly was just dismissed, and wanted to stand aside till the multitude should pass; but this human tide continues to flow, without interruption or abatement, from morn to night. Then there is such an infinity of gay equipages, coaches, chariots, chaises, and other carriages, continually rolling and shifting before your eyes, that one's head grows giddy looking at them; and the imagination is quite confounded with splendour and variety. Nor is the prospect by water less grand and astonishing than that by land: you see three stupendous bridges, joining the opposite bands of a broad, deep and rapid river; so vast, so stately, so elegant, that they seem to be the work of the giants; betwixt them, the whole surface of the Thames is covered with small vessels, barges, boats, and wherries, passing to and fro; and below the three bridges, such a prodigious forest of masts, for miles together, that you would think all the ships in the universe were here assembled. All that you read of wealth and grandeur in the Arabian Nights' Entertainment, and the Persian Tales, concerning Bagdad, Diarbekir, Damascus, Ispahan, and Samarkand, is here realized.

Ranelagh looks like the inchanted palace of a genie, adorned with the most exquisite performances of painting, carving and gilding, enlightened with a thousand golden lamps, that emulate the noon-day sun; crowded with the great, the rich, the gay, the happy, and the fair; glittering with cloth of gold and silver, lace, embroidery, and precious stones. While these exulting sons and daughters of felicity tread this round of pleasure, or regale in different parties, and separate lodges, with fine imperial tea and other delicious refreshments, their ears are entertained with the most ravishing delights of music, both instrumental and vocal. There I heard the famous Tenducci, a thing from

Italy — It looks for all the world like a man, though they say it is not. The voice, to be sure, is neither man's nor woman's; but it is more melodious than either; and it warbled so divinely, that, while I listened, I really thought myself in paradise.

At nine o'clock, in a charming moonlight evening, we embarked at Ranelagh for Vauxhall, in a wherry so light and slender that we looked like so many fairies sailing in a nutshell. My uncle, being apprehensive of catching cold upon the water, went round in the coach, and my aunt would have accompanied him, but he would not suffer me to go by water if she went by land; and therefore she favoured us with her company, as she perceived I had a curiosity to make this agreeable voyage — After all, the vessel was sufficiently loaded; for, besides the waterman, there was my brother Jery, and a friend of his, one Mr Barton, a country gentleman, of a good fortune, who had dined at our house — The pleasure of this little excursion was, however, damped, by my being sadly frighted at our landing; where there was a terrible confusion of wherries, and a crowd of people bawling, and swearing, and quarrelling: nay, a parcel of ugly-looking fellows came running into the water, and laid hold of our boat with great violence, to pull it a-shore; nor would they quit their hold till my brother struck one of them over the head with his cane. But this flutter was fully recompensed by the pleasures of Vauxhall; which I no sooner entered, than I was dazzled and confounded with the variety of beauties that rushed all at once upon my eye. Image to yourself, my dear Letty, a spacious garden, part laid out in delightful walks, bounded with high hedges and trees, and paved with gravel; part exhibiting a wonderful assemblage of the most picturesque and striking objects, pavilions, lodges, groves, grottoes, lawns, temples and cascades; porticoes, colonades and rotundos; adorned with pillars, statues, and painting: the whole illuminated with an infinite number of lamps, disposed in different figures of suns, stars, and constellations; the place crowded with the gayest company, ranging through those blissful shades, or supping in different lodges on cold collations, enlivened with mirth, freedom, and good humour, and animated by an excellent band of music. Among the vocal performers I had the happiness to hear the celebrated Mrs ——, whose voice was loud and shrill, that it made my head ake through excess of pleasure.

In about half an hour after we arrived we were joined by my uncle, who did not seem to relish the place. People of experience and infirmity, my dear Letty, see with very different eyes from those that such as you and I make use of — Our evening's entertainment was interrupted by an unlucky accident. In one of the remotest walks we were surprised with a sudden shower, that set the whole company a-running, and drove us in heaps, one upon another, into the rotunda; where my uncle, finding himself wet, began to be very peevish and urgent to be gone. My brother went to look for the coach, and found it with much difficulty; but as it could not hold us all, Mr Barton stayed behind. It was some time before the carriage could be brought up to the gate, in the confusion, notwithstanding the utmost endeavours of our new footman, Humphry Clinker, who lost his scratch periwig, and got a broken head in the scuffle. The moment we were seated, my aunt pulled off my uncle's shoes, and carefully wrapped his poor feet in her capuchin; then she gave him a mouth-ful of cordial, which she always keeps in her pocket, and his clothes were shifted as soon as we arrived at lodgings; so that, blessed be God, he escaped a severe cold, of which he was in great terror.

6   John Harvey Darrell, Chief Justice of Bermuda, November 1816.
Quoted from Scott, pp.65–66

It is to the brilliancy of decoration that Vauxhall Gardens owe their attraction. And although they may not be honoured with the encouraging applause of fashion I should not hesitate to confess the pleasure which I received from my first visit there.

On arriving at the entrance the scene which first bursts upon the sight is dazzling beyond what we usually expect from the sobriety of English taste: covered alcoves finished in Eastern style; walks which in distant prospect present some brilliant object of painting or transparency—all lighted with an innumerable quantity of small lamps which shed their twinkling lustre on all around. The trees beaded with ornaments over their branches shelter the numerous parties of men and women promiscuously wandering about in every direction and give it the semblance of a fairy scene.

In the midst of an open space is erected a building for the orchestra, fashioned after a Chinese pagoda, the musicians are arranged in successive steps and the back represents an organ. A profusion of coloured lamps, imitating flowers and branches of trees, depend from the cupola. The brilliance of the music and the gaiety of the surroundings give rise to an air of enthusiasm.

Suddenly,—a bell rings, the music ceases—away runs the whole party,—you follow, unknowing why or whither. But in spite of the tumult and chattering you shortly arrive at the end of one of the walks and perceive that fireworks are about to be let off. In a moment the whole air is ablaze,—crowns, hearts, initials, and various figures show themselves in meteoric flash and disappear, attended by sudden flashes which gleam on all sides through the wreathing smoke and culminate in a terrifically grand spectacle: the heroine of the piece appears as a rope-dancer, ascends the cord which at a considerable angle is rigged to a height of 70 or 80 feet. Through the smoke and flames she rapidly climbs the blazing pinnacle to the top where rockets seem to graze her in their course, exploding above, beneath, around her and spangling her flimsy dress with their scintillations. Every moment you expect to see the rope severed, to see her precipitated from the dizzy height. But still she supports herself like those fabled elves which ride upon the storm. When at length you turn away it is perhaps to visit the dancers who are fleetly footing it away, or the Highland clarinet, or more music,—some attraction in every quarter of the Gardens. Near the covered walks are boxes with every kind of refreshment which the season requires; and through the vistas of some avenues the transparencies have a most beautiful effect. One represented an aged person in a grotto profoundly intent upon a book which lay before him. The light behind the canvas contrasted perfectly with real branches of trees and brushwood which hung over the entrance to his retreat, and made a wonderful foil to the revelry of the scene some few hundred yards distant.

On returning to the principal saloon, oval in shape and exceedingly spacious, we found a couple exhibiting the elegance and grace of their figures in a waltz. It was impossible to have a soul at all susceptible of the enthusiasm which music, which beauty, which gracefulness of motion excite, and not to be agitated by the scene and not to feel something of that luxurious thrill of emotions which tinges our reflections with pleasurable sadness.

7 Charles Dickens, 'Sketches by Boz' (from 1830s): 'Vauxhall Gardens by Day'

There was a time when if a man ventured to wonder how Vauxhall Gardens would look by day, he was hailed with a shout of derision at the absurdity of the idea. Vauxhall, by daylight! A porter-pot without porter, the House of Commons without the Speaker, a gas-lamp without the gas—pooh, nonsense, the thing was not to be thought of. It was rumoured, too, in those times, that Vauxhall Gardens by day were the scene of secret and hidden experiments; that there, carvers were exercised in the mystic art of cutting a moderate-sized ham into slices thin enough to pave the whole of the grounds; that beneath the shade of the tall trees, studious men were constantly engaged in chemical experiments, with the view of discovering how much water a bowl of negus could possibly bear; and that in some retired nooks, appropriated to the study of ornithology, other sage and learned men were, by a process known only to themselves, incessantly employed in reducing fowls to a mere combination of skin and bone.

Vague rumours of this kind, together with many others of a similar nature, cast over Vauxhall Gardens an air of deep mystery; and as there is a great deal in the mysterious, there is no doubt that to a good many people, at all events, the pleasure they afforded was not a little enhanced by this very circumstance.

Of this class of people we confess to having made one. We loved to wander among these illuminated groves, thinking of the patient and laborious researches which had been carried on there during the day, and witnessing their results in the suppers which were served up beneath the light of lamps and to the sound of music at night. The temples and saloons and cosmoramas and fountains glittered and sparkled before our eyes; the beauty of the lady singers and the elegant deportment of the gentlemen, captivated our hearts; a few hundred thousand of additional lamps dazzled our senses; a bowl or two of punch bewildered our brains; and we were happy.

In an evil hour, the proprietors of Vauxhall Gardens took to opening them by day. We regretted this, as rudely and harshly disturbing that veil of mystery which had hung about the property for many years, and which none but the noonday sun, and the late Mr. Simpson, had ever penetrated. We shrunk from going; at this moment we scarcely know why. Perhaps a morbid consciousness of approaching disappointment – perhaps a fatal presentiment – perhaps the weather; whatever it was, we did *not* go until the second or third announcement of a race between two balloons tempted us, and we went.

We paid our shilling at the gate, and then we saw for the first time, that the entrance, if there had been any magic about it at all, was now decidedly disenchanted, being, in fact, nothing more nor less than a combination of very roughly-painted boards and sawdust. We glanced at the orchestra and supper-room as we hurried past—we just recognised them, and that was all. We bent our steps to the firework-ground; there, at least, we should not be disappointed. We reached it, and stood rooted to the spot with mortification and astonishment. *That* the Moorish tower—that wooden shed with a door in the centre, and daubs of crimson and yellow all round, like a gigantic watch-case! *That* the place where night after night we had beheld the undaunted Mr. Blackmore make his terrific ascent, surrounded by flames of fire, and peals of artillery, and where the white garments of Madame Somebody (we forget even her name now), who nobly devoted her life to the manufacture of fireworks, had so often been seen fluttering in the wind, as she called up a red, blue or parti-coloured light to illumine her temple! *That* the—but at this moment the bell rang; the people scampered away, pell-mell, to the spot from whence the sound proceeded; and we, from the mere force of habit, found ourselves running among the first, as if for very life.

It was for the concert in the orchestra. A small party of dismal men in cocked hats were 'executing' the overture to *Tancredi*, and a numerous assemblage of ladies and gentlemen, with their families, had rushed from their half-emptied stout mugs in the supper boxes, and crowded to the spot. Intense was the low murmur of admiration when a particularly small gentleman, in a dress coat, led on a particularly tall lady in a blue sarcenet pelisse and bonnet of the same, ornamented with large white feathers, and forthwith commenced a plaintive duet.

We knew the small gentleman well; we had seen a lithographed semblance of him, on many a piece of music, with his mouth wide open as if in the act of singing; a wine-glass in his hand; and a table with two decanters and four pineapples on it in the background. The tall lady, too, we had gazed on, lost in raptures of admiration, many and many a time—how different people *do* look by daylight, and without punch, to be sure! It was a beautiful duet: first the small gentleman asked a question, and then the tall lady answered it; then the small gentleman and the tall lady sang together most melodiously; then the small gentleman went through a little piece of vehemence by himself, and got very tenor indeed, in the excitement of his feelings, to which the tall lady responded in a similar manner; then the small gentleman had a shake or two, after which the tall lady had the same, and then they both merged imperceptibly into the original air: and the band wound themselves up to a pitch of fury, and the small gentleman handed the tall lady out, and the applause was rapturous.

The comic singer, however, was the especial favourite; we really thought that a gentleman, with his dinner in a pocket-handkerchief, who stood near us, would have fainted with excess of joy. A marvellous facetious gentleman that comic singer is; his distinguishing characteristics are, a wig approaching to the flaxen, and an aged countenance, and he bears the name of one of the English counties, if we recollect right. He sang a very good song about the seven ages, the first half-hour of which afforded the assembly the purest delight; of the rest we can make no report, as we did not stay to hear any more.

We walked about, and met with a disappointment at every turn; our favourite views were mere patches of paint; the fountain that had sparkled so showily by lamp-light, presented very much the appearance of a water pipe that had burst; all the ornaments were dingy, and all the walks gloomy. There was a special attempt at rope-dancing in the little open theatre. The sun shone upon the spangled dresses of the performers, and their evolutions were about as inspiriting and appropriate as a country-dance in a family vault. So we retraced our steps to the firework-ground, and mingled with the little crowd of people who were contemplating Mr. Green.

Some half-dozen men were restraining the impetuosity of one of the balloons, which was completely filled, and had the car already attached; and as rumours had gone abroad that a Lord was 'going up', the crowd were more than usually anxious and talkative. There was one little man in faded black, with a dirty face and a rusty black neckerchief with a red border, tied in a narrow wisp round his neck, who entered into conversation with everybody, and had something to say upon every remark that was made within his hearing. He was standing with his arms folded, staring up at the balloon, and every now and then vented his feelings of reverence for the aëronaut, by saying, as he looked round to catch somebody's eye, 'He's a rum 'un is Green; think o' this here being up'ards of his two-hundredth ascent; ecod, the man as is ekal to Green never had the toothache yet, nor won't have within this hundred year, and that's all about it. When you meets with real talent, and native too, encourage it, that's what I say;' and when he had delivered himself to this effect, he would fold his arms with more determination than ever, and stare at the balloon with a sort of admiring defiance of any other many alive, beyond himself and Green, that impressed the crowd with the opinion that he was an oracle.

'Ah, you're very right, sir,' said another gentleman, with his wife, and children, and mother, and wife's sister, and a host of female friends, all in the gentility of white pocket-handkerchiefs, frills, and spencers, 'Mr. Green is a steady hand, sir, and there's no fear about him.'

'Fear!' said the little man: 'isn't it a lovely thing to see him and his wife a-going up in one balloon, and his own son and *his* wife a-jostling up against them in another, and all of them going twenty or thirty mile in three hours or so, and then coming back in pochayses? I don't know where this here science is to stop, mind you; that's what bothers me.'

Here there was a considerable talking among the females in the spencers.

'What's the ladies a-laughing at, sir?' inquired the little man, condescendingly.

'It's only my sister Mary,' said one of the girls, 'as says she hopes his lordship won't be frightened when he's in the car, and want to come out again.'

'Make yourself easy about that there, my dear,' replied the little man. 'If he was so much as to move an inch without leave, Green would jist fetch him a crack over the head with the telescope, as would send him into the bottom of the basket in no time, and stun him till they come down again.'

'Would he, though?' inquired the other man.

'Yes, would he,' replied the little one, 'and think nothing of it, neither, if he was the king himself. Green's presence of mind is wonderful.'

Just at this moment all eyes were directed to the preparations which were being made for starting. The car was attached to the second balloon, the two were brought pretty close together, and a military band commenced playing, with a zeal and fervour which would render the most timid man in existence but too happy to accept any means of quitting that particular spot of earth on which they were stationed. Then Mr. Green, sen., and his noble companion entered one car, and Mr. Green, jun., and *his* companion, the other; and then the balloons went up, and the aërial travellers stood up, and the crowd outside roared with delight, and the two gentlemen who had never ascended before, tried to wave their flags, as if they were not nervous, but held on very fast all the while; and the balloons were wafted gently away, our little friend solemnly protesting, long after they were reduced to mere specks in the air, that he could still distinguish the white hat of Mr. Green. The gardens disgorged their multitudes, boys ran up and down screaming 'bal-loon;' and in all the crowded thoroughfares people rushed out of their shops into the middle of the road, and having stared up in the air at two little black objects till they almost dislocated their necks, walked slowly in again, perfectly satisfied.

The next day there was a grand account of the ascent in the morning papers, and the public were informed how it was the finest day but four in Mr. Green's remembrance; how they retained sight of the earth till they lost it behind the clouds; and how the reflection of the balloon on the undulating masses of vapour was gorgeously picturesque; together with a little science about the refraction of the sun's rays, and some mysterious hints respecting atmospheric heat and eddying currents of air.

There was also an interesting account of how a man in a boat was distinctly heard by Mr. Green, jun., to exclaim, 'My eye!' which Mr. Green, jun., attributed to his voice rising to the balloon, and the sound being thrown back from its surface into the car; and the whole concluded with a slight allusion to another ascent next Wednesday, all of which was very instructive and amusing, as our readers will see if they look to the papers. If we have forgotten to mention the date, they have only to wait till next summer, and take the account of the first ascent, and it will answer the purpose equally well.

8   'The Spectator', 10 July, 1841

The mode of entrance into the gardens, which extend over about eleven acres, is admirably calculated to enhance their ordinary effect on the first view. We step at once from the passages into a scene of enchantment, such as in our young days opened upon our eyes as we pored over the magical pages of the Arabian Nights. It were indeed worth some sacrifice of time, money and convenience, to see for once in a lifetime that view. At first, one wide-extended and interminable blaze of radiance is the idea impressed upon the dazzled beholder. As his eyes grow accustomed to the place, he perceives the form of the principal part of the gardens resolve itself into a long quadrangle, formed by four colonnades which enclose an open space with trees, called the Grove. On his right extends one of the colonnades, some three hundred feet long, with an arched Gothic roof, where the groins are marked by lines of lamps, shedding a yellow golden light, and the pendents by single crimson lamps of a larger size at the intersections. The effect of this arrangement is most superb. Near the eye, the lines or groins appear singly, showing their purpose; farther off they grow closer and closer till at some distance the entire vista looks across one of the shorter ends of the quadrangle, illuminated in a different but still more magnificent manner by a chandelier of great size, formed of coloured lamps, and by various smaller chandeliers.

Still standing in the same place (at the door of the entrance), and looking across the interior of the quadrangle called the Grove, midway is seen the lofty orchestra, glittering all over with the many-coloured light diffused from innumerable lamps. This was erected in 1735, and has itself many interesting memories attached to it, Beneath that vast shell which forms the roof or sounding-board of the orchestra many of our greatest vocalists and performers have poured forth their strains to the delight of the crowded auditory in front—Signor and Signora Storace, Mrs Billington, Miss Tyrer (now Mrs Liston), Incledon, Braham, and a host of others, at once rise to the memory.

The Grove is illuminated not only by the reflected light from the colonnades on either side and by the orchestra, but by festoons of lamps gracefully undulating along the sides of the colonnades from one end to the other. Among the other attractions of the Grove, we find immediately we step into it some beautiful plaster casts from the antique, the light colour of which forms a fine contrast with the blackness of the neighbouring trees and the solemn gloom of the sky above, which assumes a still deeper tinge when seen under such circumstances. Immediately opposite these, at the back of the short colonnade which forms this end of the Grove, with elevated arches opening upon the colonnade, is the splendid room originally called the Pavilion, now the Hall of Mirrors, a title more appropriate as marking its distinctive character, the walls being lined with looking-glass. This is the principal supper-room.

Turning the corner we enter upon the other of the two principal colonnades, which is similarly illuminated. A little way down we find an opening into the Rotunda, a very large and handsome building, with boxes, pit, and gallery in the circular part, and on one side a stage for the performance of ballets, &c. The pit forms also, when required, an arena for the display of horsemanship. At the end of this colonnade we have on the right the colonnade forming the other extremity of the Grove, hollowed out into a semicircular form, the space being fitted up somewhat in the manner of a Turkish divan.

On the left we find the more distant and darker parts of the gardens. Here the first spot that attracts our attention is a large space, the back of which presents a kind of mimic amphitheatre of trees and foliage, having in front rock-work and fountains; from one of the latter Eve has just issued, as we perceive by the beautiful figure reclining on the grass above. Not far from this place a fine cast of Diana arresting the flying hart stands out in admirable relief from the dark-green leafy background. Here too is a large building, presenting in front the appearance of the proscenium and stage of a theatre. Ballets, performances on the tight-rope, and others of a like character, are here exhibited. The purpose of the building is happily marked by the statues of Canova's dancing-girls, one of which is placed on each side of the area at the front.

At the corner of a long walk, between trees lighted only by single lamps spread at intervals on the ground at the sides, is seen a characteristic representation of Tell's cottage in the Swiss Alps. This walk is terminated by an illuminated transparency, placed behind a Gothic gateway, representing the delicate but broken shafts of some ruined ecclesiastical structure, with a large stone cross—that characteristic feature of the waysides of Roman Catholic countries. At right angles with this walk extends a much broader one, with the additional illumination of a brilliant star; and at its termination, is an opening containing a very imposing spectacle. This is a representation in a large circular basin of water, of Neptune with his trident, driving his five sea-horses abreast, which are snorting forth liquid streams from their nostrils; these in their ascent cross and intermingle in a very pleasing and striking manner. The lustrous white and great size of the figures are, like all other works of art in the gardens, admirably contrasted with the surrounding features of the place.

Passing in our way the large building erected for the convenience of filling the great balloon, and the area where the fireworks are exhibited, we next enter the Italian Walk, so called from its having been originally decorated in the formal, exact style of the walks of that country. This is a noble promenade or avenue of great length and breadth, crossed every few yards by a lofty angular arch of lamps, with festoons of the same brilliant character, hanging from it, and having statues interspersed on each side throughout. On quitting this walk at its farther extremity we find ourselves in the centre of the long colonnade opposite to that we quitted to examine the more remote parts of the garden.

The inner side of each of the long colonnades is occupied by innumerable supper-boxes, in some of which yet remain the pictures before referred to. We have scarcely had time for this hasty survey, during which too our attention has been partially drawn away by the noble music which has been playing almost without intermission since we entered the gardens, before the performances commence with a ballet in the Rotunda, relieved from its usual dulness and absurdity by the extraordinary feats of the Ravel Family, some of which set at nought all our ordinary notions of the anatomy of the body, or the laws of its locomotion. Walking, or rather hopping across the stage, on one stilt, and without any other support, at a quiet gentlemanly pace, is but one, and not the most extraordinary, of the many curious things here done. Ducrow's troop next exhibit their unrivalled skill and elegance in the management of the horse though it is no easy task to clear the pit for them, by this time crowded with spectators. The instant the equestrian performances are over a general race ensues for the stage we have mentioned as standing in another part of the gardens, where tight-rope dancing of no ordinary kind is to be exhibited. And certainly so much ease and elegance in the accomplishment of feats that appear wonderful to be accomplished at all makes us forget the uselessness of such laboriously acquired skill, or the danger with which its display is not unfrequently attended. Indeed, as we looked upon the feats done by the performers, one of them a member of the family previously noticed, we could scarcely help wondering whether after all the tight rope was not one man's natural sphere of exertion; certainly we beheld much done on the rope that we should find it difficult to imitate off.

A bell now rings, and summons us to the last and by far the most beautiful and satisfactory to our minds of the entertainments of the evening—the fire-works. Vauxhall has long been distinguished for the excellence of its displays of this elegant art; and in the hands of the present artist its reputation has been still further advanced. In the words of a recent writer, who has described one of these exhibitions so happily that we shall do better justice to what we ourselves beheld by using his language than our own,—'The fire-works of D'Ernst were one of the most superb displays of pyrotechny that we ever saw—not so much for quantity as quality; the devices were most ingenious, and the colours intensely beautiful. The showers of sparks served as a golden fringe or setting to the luminous gems that blazed in the centre, like concentric circles of ruby, emerald, and sapphire, glowing with preternatural lustre. The rockets rushed upwards as though they would reach the moon, and burst forth in showers of golden tears, silver stars, and amber balls; while some changed, as they fell, from lustrous green to burning crimson: fiery rings darted to and fro like comets, jets of fire went spinning upwards, and nests of serpents were shaken out into the air. In short, D'Ernst might achieve a Gorgon's head with snaky tresses and flaming eyeballs, as a feat of artificial fire, if he were so minded.

9   William Makepeace Thackeray, 'Vanity Fair' (1847–8), from chapter 6

The party was landed at the Royal Gardens in due time. As the majestic Jos stepped out of the creaking vehicle the crowd gave a cheer for the fat gentleman, who blushed and looked very big and mighty, as he walked away with Rebecca under his arm. George, of course, took charge of Amelia. She looked as happy as a rose-tree in sunshine.

'I say Dobbin', says George, 'just look to the shawls and things, there's a good fellow.' And so while he paired off with Miss Sedley, and Jos squeezed through the gate into the Gardens with Rebecca at his side, honest Dobbin contented himself by giving an arm to the shawls, and by paying at the door for the whole party.

He walked very modestly behind them. He was not willing to spoil sport. About Rebecca and Jos he did not care a fig. But he thought Amelia worthy even of the brilliant George Osborne, and as he saw that good-looking couple threading the walks to the girl's delight and wonder, he watched her artless happiness with a sort of fatherly pleasure. Perhaps he felt that he would have liked to have something on his own arm besides a shawl (the people laughed at seeing the gawky young officer carrying this female burthen); but William Dobbin was very little addicted to selfish calculation at all; and so long as his friend was enjoying himself, how should he be discontented? And the truth is, that of all the delights of the Gardens; of the hundred thousand *extra* lamps, which were always lighted; the fiddlers in cocked-hats, who played ravishing melodies under the gilded cockle-shell in the midst of the Gardens; the singers, both of comic and sentimental ballads, who charmed the ears there; the country dances, formed by bouncing cockneys and cockneyesses, and executed amidst jumping, thumping and laughter; the signal which announced that Madame Saqui was about to mount skyward on a slack-rope ascending to the stars; the hermit that always sat in the illuminated hermitage; the dark walks, so favourable to the interviews of young lovers; the pots of stout handed about by the people in the shabby old liveries; and the twinkling boxes, in which the happy feasters made believe to eat slices of almost invisible ham;—of all these things, and of the gentle Simpson, that kind smiling idiot, who I daresay, presided even then over the place—Captain William Dobbin did not take the slightest notice.

He carried about Amelia's white cashmere shawl, and having attended under the gilt cockle-shell, while Mrs. Salmon performed the Battle of Borodino (a savage cantata against the Corsican upstart, who had lately met with his Russian reverses)—Mr. Dobbin tried to hum it as he walked away, and found he was humming—the tune which Amelia Sedley sang on the stairs, as she came down to dinner.

He burst out laughing at himself; for the truth is, he could sing no better than an owl.

It is understood, as a matter of course, that our young people, being in parties of two and two, made the most solemn promises to keep together during the evening and separated in ten minutes afterwards. Parties at Vauxhall always did separate, but 'twas only to meet again at supper-time, when they could talk of their mutual adventures in the interval.

What were the adventures of Mr. Osborne and Miss Amelia? That is a secret. But be sure of this—they were perfectly happy, and correct in their behaviour; and as they had been in the habit of being together any time in these fifteen years, their tête-à-tête offered no particular novelty.

But when Miss Rebecca Sharp and her stout companion lost themselves in a solitary walk, in which there were not above five score more of couples similarly straying, they both felt that the situation was extremely tender and critical, and now or never was the moment, Miss Sharp thought, to provoke the declaration which was trembling on the timid lips of Mr. Sedley. They had previously been to the panorama of Moscow, where a rude fellow, treading on Miss Sharp's foot, caused her to fall back with a little shriek into the arms of Mr. Sedley, and this little incident increased the tenderness and confidence of that gentleman to such a degree, that he told her several of his favourite Indian stories over again for, at least, the sixth time.

'How I should like to see India!' said Rebecca.

'Should you?' said Joseph, with a most killing tenderness; and was no doubt about to follow up this artful interrogatory by a question still more tender (for he puffed and panted a great deal, and Rebecca's hand, which was placed near his heart, could count the feverish pulsations of that organ), when, oh, provoking! the bell rang for the fireworks, and, a scuffling and running taking place, these interesting lovers were obliged to follow in the stream of people.

Captain Dobbin had some thoughts of joining the party at supper: as, in truth, he found the Vauxhall amusements not particularly lively—but he paraded twice before the box where the now united couples were met, and nobody took any notice of him. Covers were laid for four. The mated pairs were prattling away quite happily, and Dobbin knew he was as clean forgotten as if he had never existed in this world.

'I should only be de trop,' said the Captain, looking at them rather wistfully. 'I'd best go and talk to the hermit,'—and so he strolled off out of the hum of men, and noise, and clatter of the banquet, into the dark walk, at the end of which lived that well-known pasteboard Solitary. It wasn't very good fun for Dobbin—and, indeed, to be alone at Vauxhall, I have found, from my own experience, to be one of the most dismal sports ever entered into by a bachelor.

The two couples were perfectly happy then in their box: where the most delightful and intimate conversation took place. Jos was in his glory, ordering about the waiters with great majesty. He made the salad; and uncorked the Champagne; and carved the chickens; and ate and drank the greater part of the refreshments on the tables. Finally, he insisted upon having a bowl of rack punch; everybody had rack punch at Vauxhall. 'Waiter, rack punch.'

That bowl of rack punch was the cause of all this history. And why not a bowl of rack punch as well as any other cause? Was not a bowl of prussic acid the cause of Fair Rosamond's retiring from the world? Was not a bowl of wine the cause of the demise of Alexander the Great or, at least, does not Dr. Lempriere say so?—so did this bowl of rack punch influence the fates of all the principal characters in this 'Novel without a Hero,' which we are now relating. It influenced their life, although most of them did not taste a drop of it.

The young ladies did not drink it; Osborne did not like it; and the consequence was that Jos, that fat *gourmand*, drank up the whole contents of the bowl; and the consequence of his drinking up the whole contents of the bowl was a liveliness which at first was astonishing, and then became almost painful; for he talked and laughed so loud as to bring scores of listeners around the box, much to the confusion of the innocent party within it; and, volunteering to sing a song (which he did in that maudlin high key peculiar to gentlemen in an inebriated state), he almost drew away the audience who were gathered round the musicians in the gilt scollop-shell and received from his hearers a great deal of applause.

'Brayvo, Fat un!' said one; 'Angcore, Daniel Lambert!' said another; 'What a figure for the tight-rope!' exclaimed another wag, to the inexpressible alarm of the ladies, and the great anger of Mr. Osborne.

'For Heaven's sake, Jos, let us get up and go,' cried that gentleman, and the young women rose.

'Stop, my dearest diddle-diddle-darling,' shouted Jos, now as bold as a lion, and clasping Miss Rebecca round the waist. Rebecca started, but she could not get away her hand. The laughter outside redoubled. Jos continued to drink, to make love, and to sing; and, winking and waving his glass gracefully to his audience, challenged all or any to come in and take a share of his punch.

Mr. Osborne was just on the point of knocking down a gentleman in top-boots, who proposed to take advantage of this invitation, and a commotion seemed to be inevitable, when by the greatest good luck a gentleman by the name of Dobbin, who had been walking about the gardens, stepped up to the box. 'Be off, you fools!' said this gentleman—shouldering off a great number of the crowd, who vanished presently before his cocked hat and fierce appearance—and he entered the box in a most agitated state.

'Good Heavens! Dobbins, where *have* you been?' Oborne said, seizing the white cashmere shawl from his friend's arm, and huddling up Amelia in it. 'Make yourself useful, and take charge of Jos here, whilst I take the ladies to the carriage.'

Jos was for rising to interfere—but a single push from Osborne's finger sent him puffing back into his seat again, and the lieutenant was enabled to remove the ladies in safety. Jos kissed his hand to them as they retreated, and hiccupped out 'Bless you! Bless you!' Then, seizing Captain Dobbin's hand, and weeping in the most pitiful way, he confided to that gentleman the secret of his loves. He adored that girl who had just gone out; he had broken her heart, he knew he had, by his conduct; he would marry her the next morning at St. George's, Hanover Square; he'd knock up the Archbishop of Canterbury at Lambeth: he would, by Jove! and have him in readiness; and, acting on this hint, Captain Dobbin shrewdly induced him to leave the gardens and hasten to Lambeth Palace, and, when once out of the gates, easily conveyed Mr. Jos Sedley into a hackney-coach, which deposited him safely at his lodgings.

10   On Ranelagh, from 'The Anbulator, or the Stranger's Companion in a Tour Round London' (1782)

The first and principal object that strikes the spectator is, what was formerly the grand orchestra, but is now called the fire-place, erected in the middle of the rotundo, reaching to the cieling, and at the same time supporting the roof; but it being found too high to yield to the company the full entertainment of the music, the performers were removed into another orchestra, erected in the space of one of the porticos: the former, however, still remains, an illustrious monument to the ingenuity of the artist, and is the most magnificent embellishment in the rotundo. It is a grand, beautiful, regular and complete structure, without the least dissonance or incongruity in any of its parts. It appears at first sight like a large and splendid column curiously and finely ornamented with paintings, carvings and niches.

The circular pile is formed by eight triumphal arches of the Doric order. The pillars are divided into two stories: the first are painted in the resemblance of marble, and decorated with masks, and other ornaments; and at the front of the arches are sconces on each side; over these pillars are eight flower-branches of small lamps. The pillars in the second story are fluted and gilt, and surmounted with termini of plaister of Paris. Above the eight triumphal arches was the orchestra, which is now closed up, and several musical instruments are painted round it, being emblematic of its original design: the eight compartments which are made by the termini, and were formerly open, are decorated with festoons of flowers finely painted, resembling niches with vases and statues in them. The pillars which form the eight triumphal arches are the principal support of the grand and curious roof, which for size and manner of construction is not to be equalled in Europe: the astonishing genius of the architect is here concealed from our view by the cieling; but it may easily be conceived that, such a roof could not be made and supported by any of the ordinary methods; and if the timber-works above were laid open to public view, they would strike every beholder with amazement and admiration.

The space on which this structure stands, is enclosed by a balustrade; and in the centre is one of the most curious and admirable contrivances that ever the judgement of man could frame: it consists of an elegant fire-place that cannot smoak or become offensive. In cold weather it renders the whole rotundo very warm and comfortable. The chimney has four faces, and by tins over each of them, which are taken off and put on at pleasure, the heat is either confined or permitted to exhale, as it is found most agreeable to the company; but the chief merit consists in having surmounted the many difficulties, and almost impossibilities, in erecting and fixing this fire-place, which every architect on the slightest examination will instantly perceive . . . The chimney which proceeds to the top of the rotundo is of brick.

. . . Round the rotundo are fifty two boxes for the accommodation of the company, with a table and cloth spread in each. In these the company are regaled, without any further expence, with tea or coffee. In each of these boxes is a droll painting, in the mimic masquerade or pantomime taste, and between each box hangs a bell-lamp with two candles in it . . . Before these paintings were put up, the backs were all blinds, that could be taken down and put up at pleasure; but apprehensions arising that many people might catch cold by others indiscreetly moving them at improper times, it was resolved to put up paintings, and to fix them. These paintings were made for blinds to the windows at the time of the famous masquerades: the figures at that distance looked very well, and seemed to be the size of real life; but now, being brought too near our view, they look rather preposterous. At the back of each box is a pair of folding doors, which open into the gardens . . . Each of these boxes will commodiously hold seven or eight persons.

Over the boxes is a gallery fronted with a balustrade and pillars painted in the resemblance of marble, which contains the like number of boxes, with a lamp at the front of each; and at the back is a blind that can be put up or taken down at pleasure, in order to render the boxes either airy or close, as is most agreeable to the company, and a pair of folding doors at the back of each, in the same manner as the lower ones.

At the distance of ten boxes from the orchestra on the right hand is the King's box . . .

The surface of the floor is plaister of Paris, over which is a mat, to prevent the company catching cold by walking upon it; for this amusement of walking round the rotundo may be considered as one of the pleasures of the place . . . This mat answers another very useful purpose for, if the company were to walk on boards, the noise made by their heels would be so great, that it would be impossible to hear anything else; but, the mat, being soft, not a step is perceived, and thus the music is heard in every part of the rotundo, and conversation is not interrupted by a disagreeable clangor. However, for the sake of balls, which are occasionally given here when the entertainments are over, two spaces are left unmatted from two of the porticos opposite each other to the fire-place in the centre. Formerly there were two sets of company dancing almost every night, who continued as long as they thought proper, and each was provided with a band of music from the orchestra.

The cieling is painted a kind of olive colour, and round the extremity is a rainbow. From the cieling descend twenty chandeliers in two circles; each chandelier is ornamented with a gilt crown, and the candles are contained in thirteen bell lamps, by which means they cast a more brilliant light . . . all parts shine with a resplendency, as if formed of the very substance of light; then doth the masterly disposition of the architect, the proportion of the parts, and the harmonious distinction of the several pieces, appear to the greatest advantage, the most minute part of this effulgence lying open to the inspection.

. . . The rotundo stands on higher ground than the Gardens; it is surrounded on the back part by a gravel walk, which is lighted with lamps, and at the extremity of the eminence are planted shrubs and bushes. Here is a flight of steps, which descend to a beautiful octagon grass plat that is bounded by a gravel-walk, and shaded by elm and yewtrees. Contiguous to this beautiful spot are several little serpentine walks: in the evening they are lighted with lamps, which glitter through the trees and have a pleasing effect.

But the grand, and by some esteemed the finest, walk in the whole Gardens, is at the extremity on the left hand leading from the matted avenue, or covered way, at the south end of Ranelagh-house to the bottom of the gardens. This gravel walk is decorated on each side by a grass plat shaded with yew and elm trees, and lighted with twenty lamps, projecting from the latter. On an eminence at the bottom is a circular temple dedicated to Pan . . .

On the right side of the gardens is a beautiful canal, which in a warm evening diffuses an agreeable coolness, and renders the gardens still more pleasant.

At the lower end of the canal is a grotto, below which is a pipe that communicates with the river Thames, for the use of carrying off the foul water in the canal and receiving fresh.

On each side the canal are handsome gravel-walks, lighted with lamps and shaded with trees and hedges; the latter of which are cut with the utmost exactness and look extremely neat. The walk on the left side of the canal is lighted with twelve lamps; but on the right side are two walks: that next the water is lighted with ten lamps, and the other, which runs parallel with it, with thirty four; this latter walk is a very fine and spacious one; it is shaded on both sides with lofty trees, and from each is a pleasant prospect. On the right are the gardens of Chelsea hospital, and on the left the canal and Ranelagh gardens. At the bottom of the walk are twenty lamps set in three triumphal arches, which extend from one side of the walk to the other, and in the evening, make a most charming and beautiful appearance. Here we meet the walk . . . that comes from the water, and by which the company enter the gardens.

11   On Ranelagh in 1775, from 'Sharpe's London Magazine', by F. W. Fairholt

Places of public amusement are always curious and worthy studies for such as desire to see or know the character of a nation. The visitor to the Champs Elysée and Bal Mabille, in Paris, who sees in the former place middle-aged men and women riding round and round on wooden horses, like children at a fair, or witnesses, in the latter, elderly men dancing more extravagantly than a clown in a London pantomime, will be struck with the difference in mental feeling between the two countries, which makes them as distinct as their languages. Here such scenes could not take place; they are contradictory to our natures; for the English still 'amuse themselves gravely, after the fashion of their country,' as they were described by the German traveller of the reign of Elizabeth. But amusements are not only national, they are in some degree local, depending upon peculiar tastes in peculiar places. They are even destined at times to live and die, 'the butterfly of the hour', at the caprice of the world of gaiety. How many such have been called into existence in London, and, after being 'the rage' for a time, have been suddenly deposed from Fashion's throne, to make way for some other short-lived favourite and died by a neglect as unreasonable as their temporary popularity might have been unexpected.

Such 'a sport for Fortune's wheel' was Ranelagh. Constructed at an enormous expense, with all the art and luxury of the day, a vast hall held the crowds who came, and regaled them with music, the best the world afforded; or gave them an equally luxurious garden to walk in. Its local advantages were great, situated near to London, but yet sufficiently in the outskirts to enjoy pure air, and reached easily by land or water, at a period when both modes of voyaging from the town were common, it added the still greater advantage of the almost unlimited patronage of the nobility and gentry. Even royalty smiled on Ranelagh, which rivalled the levees at the palace itself, for the rank and beauty which at times was received within its walls. Might not these walls be inscribed with *Esto perpetua?*—a few years roll away, the fickle goddess, Fashion, with her all-powerful persuasion, beckons her votaries elsewhere, who readily follow wherever she leads; and Ranelagh, the home of gaiety, the sanctum of pleasure, for which at one time those votaries would have argued or fought, loses both defender and visitor, becomes a wreck, and the next generation 'asks where the fabric stood.'

Scattered through the pages of the moralist, the novelist, and the topographer, there is much to enable us to comprehend the place in its palmy days, and resuscitate its most glowing features. Let us by their aid indulge in a Parthian glance at glories which delighted our great grandsires. Verily, book-lore is 'most excellent' to enable us to achieve such things so well.

It is a brilliant afternoon in June; it has been one of those days capable of making a foreigner satisfied with an English climate; and inspiring Londoners with that desire for a 'day out', which even so respectable a trader as John Gilpin once in his life felt . . .

On we glide, by somewhat lonely banks, till Chelsea comes in sight. What a gay little place it appears, with its mall and rows of verdant trees; but we got no further than the old hospital, that noble institution for the unrecorded worthies whose prowess made the victories of Marlborough. The platform of the hospital is to be kept open tonight, 'for the greater conveniency of disembarking'. Ranelagh is close on the London side of the hospital. See, as we approach it, how gay it looks in the twilight, lamps sparkle everywhere, it is unusually gay. What a crowd of boats press towards the steps; how people are 'hauled' out of them by the 'Jacks-in-the-water'. How unceremoniously the boats are pushed off to make way for other disembarkations. What quarrelling and abuse among the scullers; what fussing and fright among the ladies; what offended dignity among the magnates of the city; what cool nonchalance among the *Bon Ton*, who affect a perfect unconsciousness of all but their own *clique*. Let us get on shore as best we may; for hark! the music begins.

The gardens are not very large, as you see: but there are trim walks, well gravelled, and green hedgerows well trimmed; a long canal, upon which you may row in boats; or, if you have aquatic taste, you may walk from the land to a Chinese pavilion built in the centre of the lake, and which is now hung with lamps reflecting their sparkling in the water with pretty effect. To-night, however, a temporary bower for dancing has been erected around the canal. Another temporary building has also been constructed, called 'the Temple of Neptune;' it is octagonal, and lined with striped linen, of the colours of the navy; it is supported by light pillars in the centre, which are hung round with gay streamers and flags of all countries; and is lighted by lustres hanging between each pillar. There the company assemble on landing, and walk or dance in the gardens till supper-time; for the gem of Ranelagh—the Rotunda—is closed at present, and the whole day has been occupied in preparing the interior for a sumptuous repast.

Let us ramble in the garden and enjoy the gay scene. What a crowd is here! 'Like a full Ranelagh,' has become a sort of proverbial saying for a crowded fashionable assembly. We are told that there are two thousand persons present; and amongst them are the two Royal Dukes of Gloucester and Cumberland, the Duke of Northumberland, Lord North, Lyttleton, Melbourne, Cholmondeley, and 'numerous others too tedious to mention', with their respective ladies, whose beauty and bright looks might banish tedium for ever. The French, Spanish, Prussian, Russian, and Neapolitan ambassadors are here. In fact, 'all the world,' as the beautiful leader of fashion, Lady Almeria Carpenter, would say, who is also present, gay and brilliant as ever. But this is no wonder, for Mrs. Cornely, of Carlisle-house, Soho, the *arbitress elegantiarum* of the *élite*, is supreme ruler here for the night; she has been allowed seven hundred guineas, to be expended in supper and decorations; so we may expect something striking.

And is it not striking? Dr. Johnson, that veritable *ursa major*, declared, on his first visit, the 'the *coup d'oeil* was the finest thing he had ever seen.' He has said to Sir Adam Ferguson, with much true philosophy, 'I am a friend to public amusements, for they keep people from vice.' With no taste for the country, he admires a crowd of well-mannered persons enjoying themselves, and when his friend Boswell, with Scottish philosophy, doubted if there was half-a-guinea's worth of pleasure in seeing such a place, at once answered, 'But, sir, there is half-a-guinea's worth of inferiority in not having seen it.' And when Boswell querulously replied, 'I doubt, sir, whether there are many happy people here,' the Doctor at once 'settled' him by declaring, 'Yes, sir, there are many happy people here. There are many people here who are watching hundreds, and who think hundreds are watching them.'

The Doctor's reply was an exceedingly happy one, for the pleasure of seeing, and being seen, is one of the great inducements to visiting Ranelagh in general, as a promenade concert in the Rotunda is the only thing afforded in the way of amusement on ordinary occasions. Smollett has described it in its best colours in his *Humphrey Clinker:*—'Ranelagh looks like the enchanted palace of a geni, adorned with the exquisite performances of painting, carving, and gilding; enlightened with a thousand golden lamps, that emulate the noon-day sun; crowded with the gay, the rich, the happy, and the fair; glittering with cloth of gold and silver lace, embroidery and precious stones. While these exulting sons and daughters of felicity tread this round of pleasure, or regale, in different parties and separate lodges, with fine imperial tea, and other delicious refreshments, their ears are entertained with the most ravishing delights of music, both instrumental and vocal.'

It has always been a great place for settling fashions in dress; the 'Ranelagh mob-cap' was first introduced here, and ladies' magazines are generally full of pictures and descriptions of 'dresses as worn at Ranelagh.'

The monotony has been sometimes termed 'dull:' so it is said to be by Captain Mirvan in Miss Burney's capital novel *Evelina;* but the fashionable Mr. Lovel quietly replies, that it wants 'something *d'un vrai gout* to be really sensible of its merit. Those whose connexions, and so forth, are not among *les gens comme il faut,* can feel nothing but *ennui* at such as place as Ranelagh.'

To prevent such a feeling now, let us sit down and recount its history, for we have seen all that is to be seen till supper-time. Ranelagh-House, Chelsea, was the residence of the Earl of Ranelagh, the mansion having been built about 1690, and the grounds laid out upon land originally belonging to the Royal Hospital here. It was one of those solid, Dutch-looking houses, fashionable in the reign of William III., whose stolidity pervaded national taste, (or rather the *want of taste* which passed for it,) at the end of that eventful century. The gardens were equally formal, with square beds and straight walks, and chilling monotony. At the earl's decease, in 1712, his daughter was installed mistress of the mansion. She sold it, in 1733, to 'an eminent builder,' named Timbrell, for £3,200, and this 'eminent' person resold it in lots. Lacy, the patentee of Drury-lane, now came into the field, in conjunction with one of those foreign purveyors of popular pleasures who live here by their wits, named Rietti, and the worthy couple at once took a lease of the premises; their ideas soared far above Vauxhall; they determined to eclipse it, and produce a place of amusement more suitable to an English climate—a garden, like Vauxhall, which should also contain within its area a covered hall, of a size and splendour unknown before to England. Their ideas were more expansive than their means; but, with knowledge and tact, they appealed to the gay world as share-holders; the project 'took well,' the property was divided into thirty-six shares, and the great Rotunda built, and gardens laid out anew. It was first opened in 1752, with the greatest *éclat*. 'A public breakfast' was the novelty hit upon for the opening; but the magistrates of London and Westminster, horrified at this outburst of fashionable extravagance 'in broad daylight', succeeded in suppressing such doings by act of parliament, as detrimental to society. The next novelty was 'morning concerts', for the fashionable world, having discovered that pleasure might begin early in the day, determined not to be baulked by trifles; but, prudently wishing to 'muzzle the magistrates,' they selected their music at first chiefly from oratorios. It was 'only a little sacred music' that led the way to 'secularities' of a more questionable character. I need not mention catch-club effusions; what are they to masquerades, which have been held here in all their riotousness? Certainly the present age is very corrupt in high quarters. The Duchess of Kingston has appeared at the Pantheon as Iphegenia, 'undressed for the sacrifice,' in a loose clothing of gauze. Colonel Watson, of the Guards, has figured at Mrs. Cornely's as Adam, 'in flesh-coloured silk, with an apron of fig-leaves;' and Colonel Luttrell as 'a dead corpse in a shroud', dragging his coffin after him. The changes of manners may lead to much serious reflection; the history of a public garden to deep thought on public morality—the vicissitudes of the present one to much curious narration; but I find I am unable 'to bestow all my tediousness on your worship,' for it is half-past ten o'clock, and see, the Rotunda is thrown open, and the crowning point of the evening awaits us.

The exterior, as you will perceive, has something of the character of the old Roman in it. It has been compared to the Pantheon. It measures externally one hundred and eighty feet in diameter, the interior being some thirty feet less. An arcade runs entirely round the lower story on the outside; and over this is an open gallery, sheltered by a slated covering, which projects from the body of the Rotunda. Above this are sixty windows, which light the interior by day. The roof, which rises above—a sort of flattened sphere—is considered a model of constructive art. There are four Doric porticos opposite each other, by which the company enter. Let us crowd in with the rest. Is not this the *coup d'oeil* worthy of Dr. Johnson's praises?

The vast circular hall is brilliantly lighted with parti-coloured lamps, tastefully arranged, depending from the roof, or hanging in festoons in front of the arched boxes which surround the building below, and are appropriated to tea and supper parties. At the back of these boxes you will perceive some droll and characteristic paintings, by some of our better-class artists, not by mere sign-painters, though that class of art, being now extensively patronised and well paid, numbers many clever men in its ranks. You will see that the pillars which divide each box rise upward, and form a support to the roof; and that every alternate pillar is decorated from top to bottom with an oblong looking-glass in a gilt frame. A door leads from each box into the gardens. In front of every box is a large bell-shaped lamp. Above the boxes is a gallery, which runs round the building; it has a balustrade of imitation marble, and this gives admission to the same number of boxes as are below. The royal box is on this stage, and is decorated with fancy paper and the crest of the Prince of Wales. Terminal figures support the roof, which, in its turn, supports twenty-three chandeliers, these add their light to the festoons of lamps already noticed; each chandelier is ornamented with a gilt coronet, and the candles are grouped in seventeen bell lamps. The orchestra occupies the centre of the building, and the ceiling arches from it like a palm-tree, and by its form assists the effect of the music; it is covered with paintings of allegorical figures and festoons of flowers. To-night, one of the finest and fullest bands of vocal and instrumental performers ever collected within these walls will play. They are to be led by Giardino, and open with a new grand piece composed for the occasion; after which various catches and glees will be sung by Messrs. Vernon, Reinhold, &c.

I can't say much for 'the poetry' of the songs usually sung at Ranelagh, although executed by our most famous singers. They are all of the milk-maiden school, and abound in fashionable pastoral. The Clelia's and Delia's, and crooks and brooks, jingle eternally in your ears, and however pretty the tune or the singer, become tedious ere long. Sometimes, however, the male singers favour us with a moral satire. Thus, a few years ago, when 'the rage' in fashion consisted of ladies appearing here in riding habits, with men's jackets and waistcoats, neckerchief and hats, Mr. Beard boldly sang a song commencing thus:—

> 'Ye belles and ye flirts, and yet pert little things,
> Who trip in this frolicsome round;
> Prithee tell me from whence this indecency springs,
> The sexes at once to confound.
> What means the cock'd hat, and the masculine air,
> With each motion design'd to perplex?
> Bright eyes were intended to languish, not stare,
> And softness the test of your sex.
> Dear girls!'

They also contrive to say something in favour of their own nonsense-verses at times, when other folk's nonsense threatens to drive it from the field. The Italian Opera has been a sad source of trouble, and they once got up a burlesque of that style of music here; a comic ode, in which Skeggs and Rooker made mockery of Italian singers, and the affair ended by this 'moral exhortation':—

> 'Let them walk, trot, or gallop, but send them from hence,
> Nor to *sound*, my dear countrymen, sacrifice *sense*;

Our wit is invaded, resist now or never,
And defend common sense and Old England for ever.'

They seemed to forget how often sense had already been sacrificed to sound by themselves. The foreigners, however, as you see, have triumphed, and we shall hear some in this orchestra to-night. Hark! they are tuning their instruments to play during supper. Suppose we try for a seat.

Well, the music is good, but the supper indifferent, and the wine very scarce. It has disappointed all, and thrown doubts on Madam Cornely's honesty, as so large a sum was allowed for expenses. Yet some few gentlemen seem to be getting very noisy, and to be paying for too much extra wine after supper; numbers have left the Rotunda for the temple in the gardens, where they will dance minuets and cotillions till the morning. Being a clear moonlight night, we had better return by water, for the land journey is a little dangerous over the lonely fields. Nay, I see by the papers that some of the aristocracy have been stopped and robbed, passing by the lonely Park wall into Piccadilly.

The dull monotony of Ranelagh in the end tired its visitors. Poor Bloomfield has described it at the close of the last century.

'To Ranelagh once in my life
By good-natured force I was driven;

What wonders were here to be found,
That a clown might enjoy or disdain!
First, we traced the gay circle all round;
Ay—and then we went round it again!'

Soon afterwards the Rotunda was pulled down, and the gayest of fashionable localities became a lonely spot. Let our second day at Ranelagh be devoted to an examination of the present aspect of this once-favoured locality.

Keeping in the line of the road from Pimlico to Chelsea, as we approach the Thames, the road takes a sudden bend to the right at Bridge-row, taking the name of Kemp's-row, which consists but of a few houses, until we approach a narrow lane, whose title, Avery Farm-row, speaks of 'fresh fields' and years gone by, when farms existed and paved streets were unknown here. The row of houses opposite is called Ranelagh-terrace, and on one side of it is Ranelagh-grove, (so called, we suppose, from the entire absence of trees,) which leads to the house and grounds occupying theposition of the famed old gardens; and on the other side is a street of small houses, termed the Commercial-road. It leads into a district unvisited by all but those whom business may carry thither; it is covered by saw-mills and factories, and the road speedily ends in a muddy, desert-like piece of land, washed by the Thames. The canal on one side, and the Ranelagh sewer on the other, have left this tract in isolated neglect. The progress of building has now crept all round it, but there is no trace of improvement here. It is something between a field, a morass, and a dust-ground, possessing characteristics of each; on one side great piles of wood are thrown, and all 'trespassers' are warned from the unfenced locality where they repose. Dirty stagnant ponds are before you, and irregular heaps of mould; pigs travel and examine the latter; a flock of ducks make themselves happy in the former. There is one trait of modern civilization alone—a solitary gas-lamp in the midst of the waste,

> 'Making night hideous'

by feebling shadowing forth the darkness elsewhere. Some unfortunates reside at the works established at the other side of the desert, in the mud of the Thames. We should think transportation infinitely more cheerful, particularly if, after a year or two's good conduct, free tickets to the Californian diggings are given. But stay! surely something of that kind is going on here. What mean these embankments, each enclosing a small pond of water, where many busy men are stationed in fishing-boots, up to their ancles in mud, shovelling the earth into sieves, and washing it, as 'the cradlers' do the auriferous mould of California. A shed is erected for some to work in, but the generality labour in the open air. On inquiry, we find that they are washing the slimy mud from the Thames, which is brought in carts at low tide, and emptied beside them; and they thus obtain a deposit of that dirty-brown sand so much in request by stone-masons, who use it to aid their saws in cutting their stone into layers or slabs. Thus there is wealth in all things where industry will seek its reward. And gold may thus be extracted from Thames mud!

If we cross the sedgy ground, we shall reach a high embankment to the left, where a stream seems to run. Alas! it has no

> 'Banks with peonied and lilied brim.'

It is a veritable London sewer, wide enough for a small river, and flowing with water, as we look down into it from the bank; it absolutely runs into the thickest population of Chelsea uncovered! And yet we have boards of health, and pretend to fear cholera!

Such 'charming banks' bound the site of old Ranelagh. This 'stream' empties itself close by the fine old landing place of Chelsea Hospital, now hardly used, but once the gay and noisy scene of debarkation for the gay, the beautiful, the titled, and the dissipated—the thousand and one who made this the focus of luxurious merriment. There is a large mansion where the Rotunda formerly stood; it looks from this point as if seated in a hollow. There is a fine cedar in the grounds, and a good avenue of old trees, where many of the gay have once disported. A pond is beside the avenue; is it a part of the old canal? Between this house and the grounds of Chelsea College, whose long avenue of trees (the old formal ponds on each side of which are now being filled up) led to the water gate, is a little tract of ground recovered from old Ranelagh, and devoted to the use of the aged pensioners. The long line of old trees, reaching diagonally from the Hospital towards the river, is one of the 'walks' of the far-famed seat of gaiety and fashion; and the curious observer may yet see fragments of lamp irons in their rugged stems, used in illuminating Ranelagh on festive nights. They are the last mementoes of gaieties for ever gone. And where the frivolous and the vain paraded in all the emptiness of fashionable folly; where the killer of time resorted to dissipate *ennui*; where the citizen came to see the *beau monde*, and his wife to study fashions; where the finest artists in music congregated, and the heaviest of philosophers, in Dr. Johnson, amused himself equally with Oliver Goldsmith, glorious in his 'bloom-coloured coat,' in an awkward attempt to 'do the fashionable;' where we can almost reenact, 'in the mind's eye,' the vivid scenes of Smollett, Richardson, and Miss Burney, as their authors describe them,—now rests the aged warrior, and trains his little garden plot; for Lord John Russell obtained for their use this piece of land, and lotted it among the old men, who, like Cincinnatus of old, find relief in such relaxation. The pretty and commodious thatched summer-house on the elevated ground is also for their use; and here they may overlook their domain, and watch between the trees the shining river and its busy steamers, which so incessantly ruffle the surface. Happy and grateful, these aged warriors creep about old Ranelagh; the ground had never more cheerful tenants. Is not the frivolity of its past uses compensated by the more noble consecration of its present one?